John Harvey Gothic England

Romance & Legend of Chivalry
A. R. Hope Moncrieff

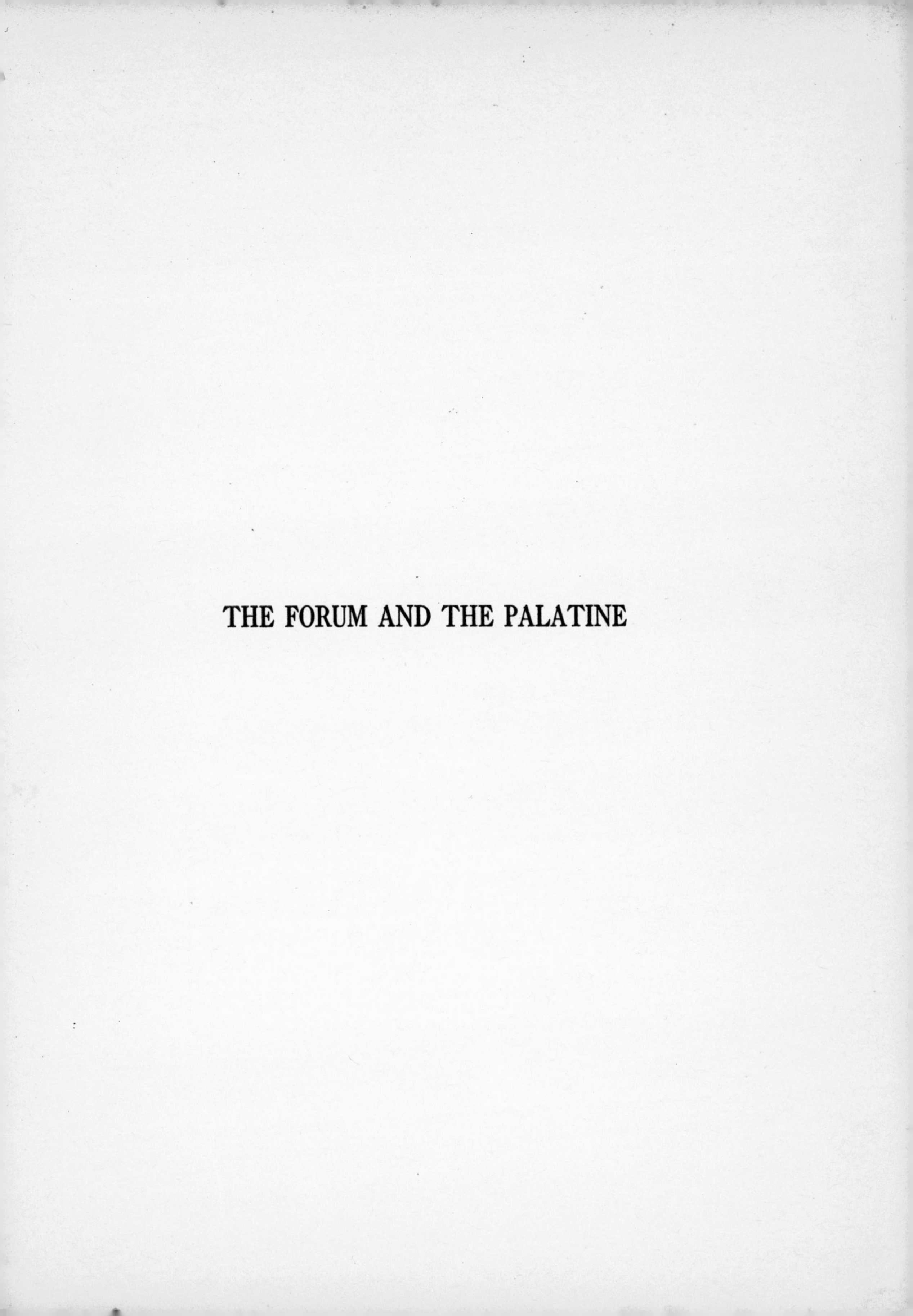

THE FORUM AND THE PALATINE

OTHER PUBLICATIONS BY THE SAME AUTHORS

CH. HUELSEN

Bilder aus der Geschichte des Kapitols. Rome, Loescher, 1899

Topographie der Stadt Rom im Alterthum (Jordan I, 3). Berlin, Weidmann, 1907

La pianta di Roma dell'Anonimo Einsidlense. Rome, Loescher, 1907

La Roma antica di Ciriaco d'Ancona. Rome, Loescher, 1907

Saggio di Bibliografia ragionata delle piante iconografiche e prospettiche di Roma dal 1551 al 1748. Rome, 1915

Römische Antikengärten des XVI. Jahrhunderts. Heidelberg, Winter, 1917

Le Chiese di Roma nel Medio Evo. Florence, Olschki, 1927

—— AND H. KIEPERT

Formae Urbis Romae antiquae, 2nd ed. Berlin, D. Reimer, 1912

—— AND H. EGGER

Die Römischen Skizzenbücher von Marten van Heemskerck im Königlichen Kupferstichkabinett zu Berlin. Bd. I, Berlin, Bard, 1913
Bd. II, ib., 1916

—— AND P. LINDNER

Die Alliaschlacht. Rome, Loescher, 1890

—— E. FIECHTER AND F. TOEBELMANN

Römische Gebälke, I. Heidelberg, Winter, 1924

HELEN H. TANZER

The Villas of Pliny the Younger. New York, Columbia University Press, 1924

THE FORUM AND THE PALATINE

BY

CHRISTIAN HUELSEN

Translated by

HELEN H. TANZER

Associate Professor of Classics at Hunter College of the City of New York

FROM THE FIRST GERMAN EDITION, WITH NUMEROUS ADDITIONS AND REVISIONS BY THE AUTHOR

WITH 30 ILLUSTRATIONS IN THE TEXT,
65 PLATES AND 1 FOLDING PLAN

NEW YORK
A. BRUDERHAUSEN
1928

TRANSLATOR'S PREFACE

This book is not merely a translation of the *Forum und Palatin,* which was published in 1926, but a new edition, as Professor Huelsen read the translation through twice, once in manuscript and the second time in proof, making extensive changes and numerous suggestions both verbal and topographical. His emendations and additions add greatly to the value of the book. Furthermore, his fifteen pages of references to Sources and Recent Literature will be invaluable to the student of Roman Topography who wishes to make a detailed study of the monuments and their remains.

My thanks are due to Professor William A. Boring, Head of the School of Architecture at Columbia University, who kindly read the translation through in manuscript in order to pass upon the technical architectural terms, to Professor David M. Robinson, Professor of Archaeology at the Johns Hopkins University, and finally to my friend and colleague at Hunter College, Professor Margaret B. Wilson, who assisted greatly in the reading of the proofs.

HELEN H. TANZER.

NEW YORK, December, 1927

CONTENTS

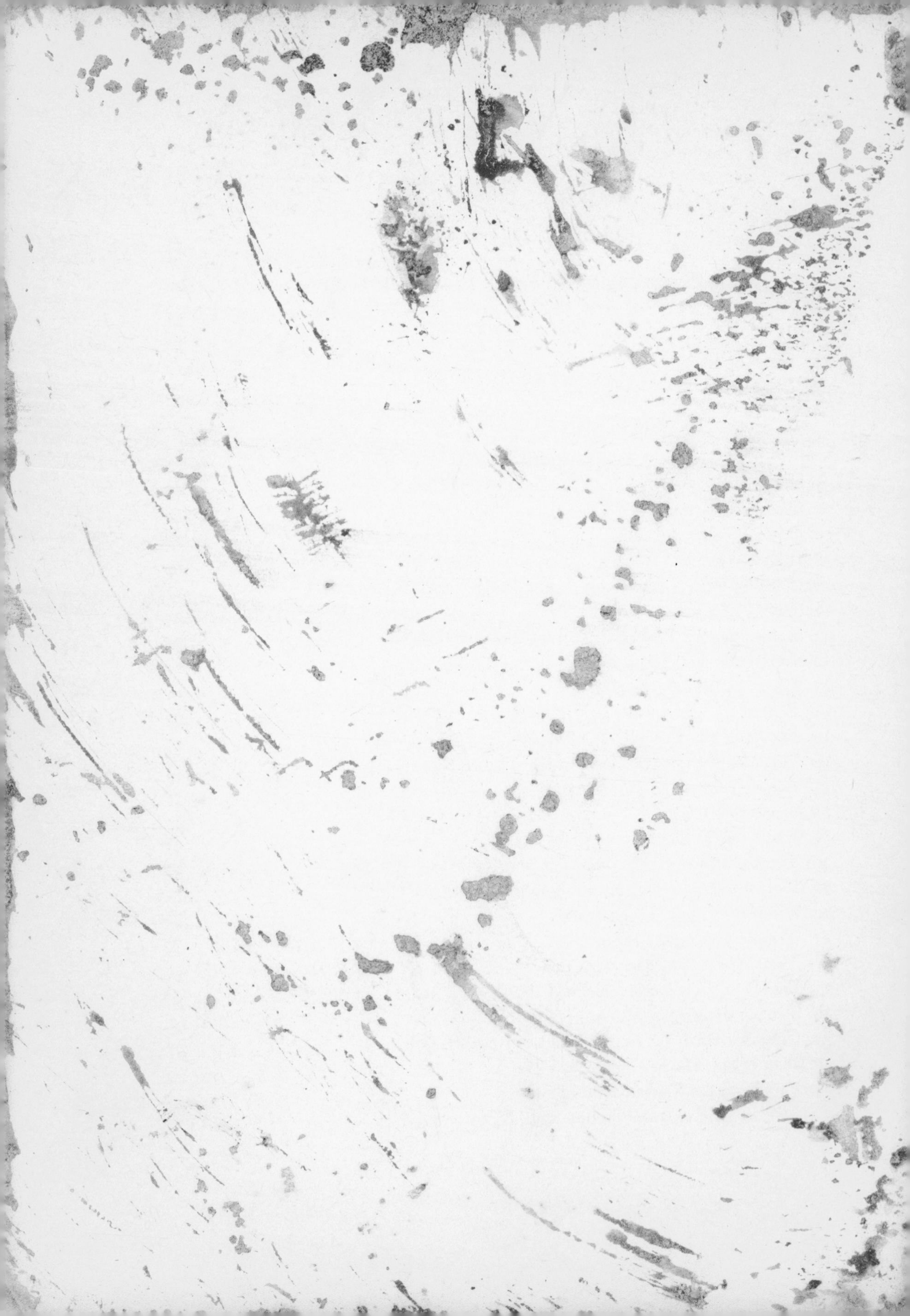

LIST OF ILLUSTRATIONS

NOTE: The illustrations marked Figs. 1–30 are scattered through the text; those marked plates 1–64 are grouped together at the back of the volume.

LIST OF ILLUSTRATIONS

PLATES

LIST OF ILLUSTRATIONS

PLATES

LIST OF ILLUSTRATIONS

PLATES

NOTE: The long axis of the Forum runs about from N. W. to S. E., but for the sake of simplicity in the text the northeast side (with the Basilica Aemilia) is referred to as the north side, and the southwest side (with the Basilica Julia), as the south side. Similarly, the four corners of the Palatine correspond approximately to the four cardinal points of the compass: the east corner lies opposite the Colosseum, the north corner toward the Forum, the west corner toward the Tiber and the south corner opposite the Aventine.

THE FORUM BEFORE IMPERIAL TIMES

WHEN the first fortified city was founded on the Palatine in place of scattered settlements—the Roma Quadrata of Romulus as Roman legend calls it—the defenses of the hill were increased because it was bordered in the direction of the Aventine and the Capitoline by low, marshy land traversed by winding brooks. Even when the so-called City of Romulus was enlarged toward the south and the east and took in the Caelian and the Esquiline, the valley between the Palatine and the Capitoline was still excluded from the city of the living. But in those days there was a burial ground at the east end on the slope of the spur of the Palatine known as the Velia, and even in later times the Romans had an inviolable law which forbade the burial or the cremation of the dead within the consecrated precincts of a city. It was not indeed until the Palatine City of the Latins had been united with the Sabine settlement on the Quirinal and the Viminal that this valley became a part of the City. The two communities then selected the Capitoline Hill, which at that time was still a spur of the Quirinal, both as the site of the highest sanctuary (temple of Jupiter Optimus Maximus Capitolinus) and as their common citadel (Arx).

The brook was dammed up and partly covered over and in course of time became the Cloaca Maxima; while the cemetery was abandoned and filled in so that even in later antiquity the memory of it had completely passed from the minds of men.

Only the most recent excavations, since 1902, have uncovered this very ancient necropolis, the beginnings of which antedate the traditional founding of Rome (753 B.C.). It has of course not been possible to keep exposed to view the graves which lie five or six metres below the imperial level. The condition of the burial place soon after the excavation is shown

The illustrations marked Figs. 1-30 are scattered through the text; those marked plates 1-64 are grouped together at the back of the volume.

in plate 1, which is reproduced from a photograph taken from the top of the temple of Faustina.

The graves were intended partly as incineration and partly as inhumation graves. The former, which were older, were circular pits cut into the native tufa, into which was set a large somewhat spherical terra cotta jar (dolium) containing the ossuary, sometimes in the form of a hut, as well as smaller vessels and other objects. In the oblong inhumation graves the bodies were generally simply laid in the graves and only a few were in primitive coffins made by hollowing out tree trunks. In both kinds of graves the offerings, clay vases, bronze weapons, fibulae and the like are very simple in design. There are no noble metals and no Greek importations with the exception of a few unpretentious examples in the more recent graves.

There may have been a similar necropolis in most ancient times at the opposite end of the valley at the declivity of the Capitoline. In the vicinity of the Umbilicus Urbis Romae (see below, p. 22) may still be seen numerous round and angular cavities cut into the native tufa which are not essentially different from those of the cemetery at the Velia. Here the cult of Vulcan, dating back to earliest times, was also localized, "not the cult of the Greek god of the smithy, the tinker, but that of the dread deity of fire, of the divine lightning as well as of the blazing flames which are productive of both good and evil." (v. Duhn, Italische Gräberkunde, I, 1924, p. 415.) It is a plausible conjecture that this is the site of the oldest Roman crematory.

Roman legend ascribes to Romulus the founding of the so-called Vulcanal adjoining the arch of Septimius Severus (see below, p. 22, and Fig. 8); and not far away from it was a mysterious monument which was shown even as late as the time of Cicero and Caesar and was supposed by most people to be the grave of the Founder of the city. A black stone, *Lapis Niger,* say the ancient authors, stood upon it; and beside it, as guardians of the tomb, were two stone lions; there was also an inscription, but in characters so archaic that even in those days some scholars took it to be the name of Faustulus, the foster father of the Founder of the city, and others, that of Hostus Hostilius, the father of the third king. In later antiquity, after Augustus, there was no further mention of this so-called grave of Romulus.

But precisely in the neighborhood where, according to ancient accounts, we might expect to find this monument—"at the boundary of the Forum and the Comitium"—recent excavations (1899) brought to light an extremely interesting group of monuments dating back to a very early age. Scarcely fifty metres distant from the Vulcanal, below the arch of Septimius Severus, and almost two metres beneath the imperial pavement were found two oblong tufa pedestals (Fig. 1, A, B), between them a single block of tufa (C), at the side a column or round pedestal (G) and a rectangular stone, *cippus* (H), also of tufa, covered on all sides with extremely archaic characters. Only about the lower half of the column

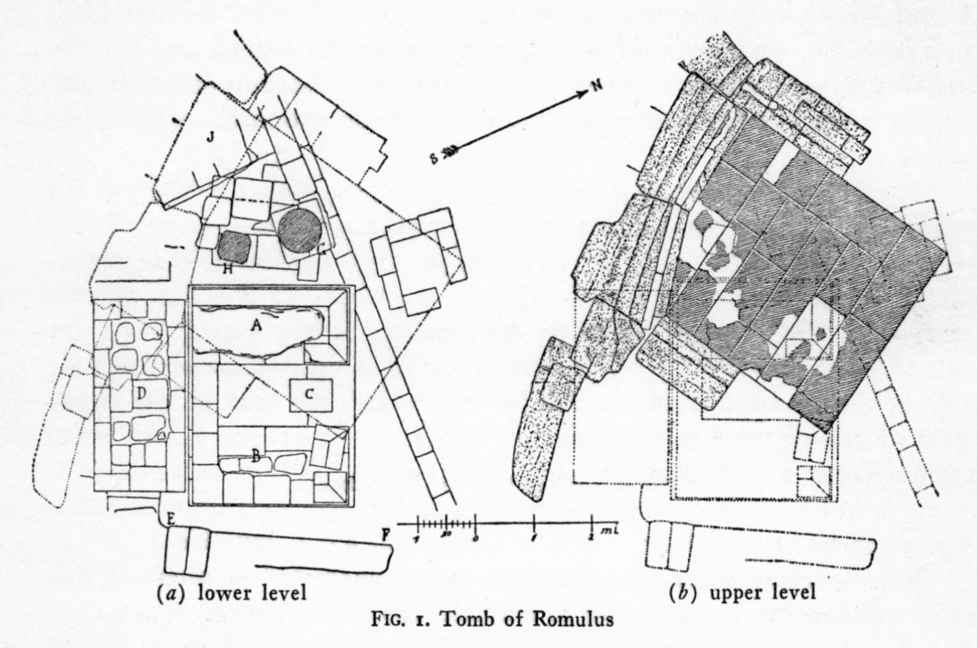

(*a*) lower level (*b*) upper level

FIG. 1. Tomb of Romulus

and the cippus are preserved (Fig. 2), both were purposely mutilated in antiquity. Nevertheless there can be no doubt that the remains belong to the same monument which was pointed out in the first century B.C. as the grave of Romulus.

On the two oblong pedestals, two lions such as are not seldom found on Etruscan and on old Italic tombs probably reclined; the tufa block between the lions may be considered as the support for a stone in the shape of a nine-pin or a pine cone made of black basalt or touchstone, quite similar to stones and pedestals found in Etruria and now in museums, e.g. in the Museo Archeologico in Florence.

The marks on the cippus (plate 19, above) which were read by some as FOSTLUS and by others as HOSTIUS or were thought to refer to Romulus are no longer visible, but then only half of the stone remains; still, judging from the form of the letters the inscription is farther removed from later Latin and is more similar to Greek (and Etruscan) inscriptions than any other. The arrangement of the writing alone is proof of great antiquity, for the lines read alternately from below up and from above down. The content of the inscription is obscure, and it will always remain so. Among the few intelligible words there is one of which the meaning seems clear: *regei,* to the king; and we may therefore consider this as the only inscription dating from the period of the Kings, which closed in 510 B.C.

The entire group, as was mentioned above, was purposely mutilated in antiquity. It has been suggested that this mutilation can be connected

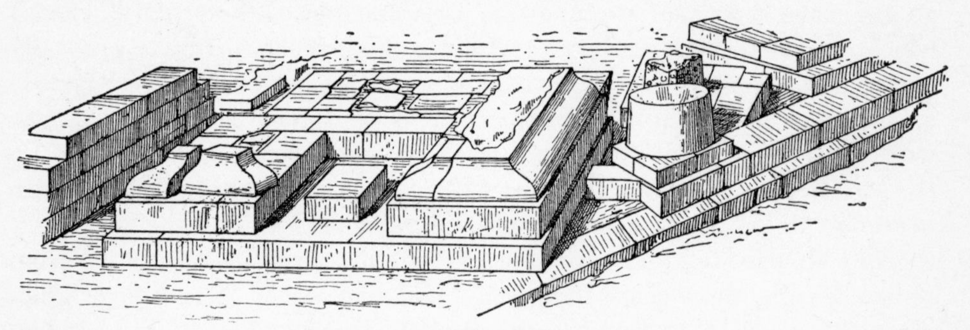

FIG. 2. Tomb of Romulus, lower level

with the capture of Rome by the Gauls (390 B.C.), but this is certainly an error, as the Celts were naturally more interested in plundering the town than in taking the trouble to mutilate historic monuments; and besides, the monuments were in a fairly complete state of preservation three hundred years later. It is more probable that the mutilation took place at the time when the pavement of the Forum was raised at the beginning of the Empire. At this time the legend that the Founder of the city had been transported to heaven by his father Mars in a fiery chariot, had become, so to speak, a dogma, and there was no longer any object in pointing out a tomb of Romulus at the most conspicuous spot in the Forum. So for three hundred years the monument remained buried and forgotten until the Emperor Maxentius, who seems to have had a particular veneration for Romulus, restored it (about 310 A.D.). At that time a spot above the old monument was paved with black marble (plate 2), not exactly above it, however, but rather with orientation toward the entrance of the Curia which Diocletian restored in 305 A.D. A white marble railing surrounded it, the foundations of which are still preserved; two large marble pedestals with inscriptions probably stood near-by. One of them, still standing in the vicinity, was dedicated by Maxentius himself to "Mars and the founders of the Eternal City," and a fragment of the other, which exactly corresponded to the first, extolling the emperor as a man of "ancient worth and singular piety," has been incorporated in the Basilica Julia in modern times.

Near the Vulcanal on the slope of the Capitol we find a third very ancient monument, the Tullianum. This was originally the well house of the Capitoline Citadel; a chamber of irregular plan, with one straight wall formed of large tufa blocks joined to a structure somewhat larger than a semicircle made of large blocks of peperino. This structure dates back to an age when the art of vaulting was as yet unknown; the peperino blocks, which are fitted together very carefully without mortar, project gradually toward the top, thus forming originally a sort of beehive structure almost as high as it was broad with an aperture at the summit. We are familiar with a similar method of construction in archaic monuments in Greece, e.g. the so-called Treasury of Atreus at Mycenae, and in Etruria; but one much nearer to Rome is the old well house on the citadel at Tusculum.

The Roman well house contained a bubbling spring, *tullus,* dating from remotest antiquity, whence the name Tullianum, but in later Roman times when the word tullus had become obsolete the founding of the building was ascribed to Tullus Hostilius, the third king. The water was dipped out originally through the opening at the summit, while the surplus flowed down to the Cloaca Maxima through a channel cut into the tufa which still exists.

Somewhat later, but still in republican times, the spring on the citadel was no longer used, perhaps because the flow was less plentiful—today it is nearly dry—and the building received a new designation—it became a dungeon, principally for those condemned to death, in which executions also took place. So that it was here that Jugurtha met his end (104 B.C.), as well as the members of the Catilinarian conspiracy (63 B.C.), Vercingetorix (46 B.C.) and other enemies of Rome. Then as early as the third century B.C. a prison, *carcer,* was constructed, the only one in Rome, adjoining the dungeon, built in part from the old quarries, *lautumiae,* near the Capitol, and consisting of numerous chambers.

During the reign of Tiberius the upper prison was rebuilt, and there are still considerable remains of this restoration (Fig. 3). The uppermost strata of the old well house were removed and the primitive pointed cupola was replaced by a flat vaulted roof (plate 3). A large trapezoidal chamber was erected over the Tullianum and the inscription on the façade toward the Comitium, which is still in a good state of preservation, bears the names of the Consuls C. Vibius Rufinus and M. Cocceius Nerva, who restored the building by a decree of the Senate. Several adjoining chambers on the north side have been explored but are not accessible.

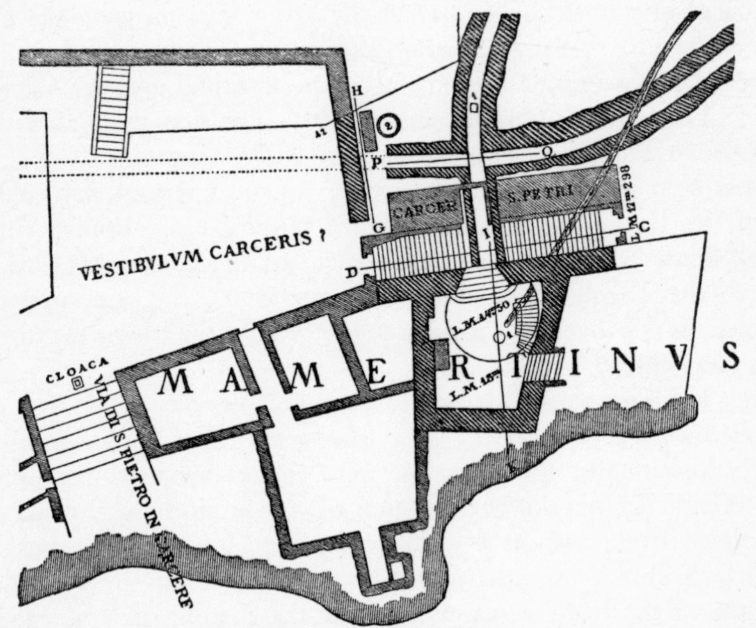

FIG. 3. Carcer Mamertinus

The Carcer kept its character to the close of the ancient period; as late as the middle of the fourth century, indeed, under Christian emperors, we hear about executions in the Tullianum. It was not until after the year 1000 A.D. that Christian legend connected the names of the Apostles Peter and Paul with the building, though in the time of Charlemagne the *Carcer S. Petri* was thought to be on the Janiculum near the Vatican. The church of S. Petri et Pauli in Carcere, in which they were supposed to have baptized their jailers Processus and Martinianus, is not mentioned before the end of the 14th century; it occupied the two ancient chambers. Above them, at the modern street level, the Oratorio del Crocefisso arose in the 16th century, and above the latter the Brotherhood of Wood Workers built first a little wooden church in 1540 which was replaced in 1598 by a more distinguished structure in the baroque style by G. B. Montano. This building is thus the only one in Rome to present four different places of worship one above the other (Fig. 4).

The Tullianum belonged originally more to the Capitol than to the Forum; it is probable that it existed for a long time before the valley was built up and while it was still outside the city limits. But then came the time, as was mentioned above, when the Latin settlement on the Palatine with its earliest market place, Forum Boarium, at the side of the hill facing the Tiber, and the Sabine settlement on the Quirinal and the Capitol felt the need of a place that would unite them. The first thing they did was to fill in the brook that flowed through the valley from the Campagna and to cover it over in some spots, though of course it remained visible in the centre of the Forum as late as the third century B.C. Roman tradition, as is well known, ascribes the establishment of the Cloaca Maxima to the dynasty of the Tarquins and the sixth century B.C., the same period, that is, in which, as is proved by the finds in the graves, the use of the necropolis at the Velia ceased.

In the territory thus acquired for building various public and private structures arose, at first at the foot of the two hills lying opposite each other, then gradually spreading out into the valley until they met and united. At the declivity of the Palatine not far from the old burial ground the temple of Vesta with its ever burning sacred fire was built, perhaps on the site of a still older sanctuary. In its vicinity was the shrine of Juturna, the nymph of the healing water. Beside the temple of Vesta according to the legend, Numa Pompilius, the second king, the organizer of all sacred customs and usages, built his palace, the Regia. On the slope of the Capitoline an area where the people could assemble, the Comitium, was marked off in a space ninety metres square, oriented to the cardinal points of the compass. To the west of the Comitium lay the Tullianum. At the north the town hall, Curia, was erected, in which the Senate assembled, and at the south where the area joined the Forum lay the oldest speakers' platform beside the so-called grave of Romulus. Farther down, where the brook entered the Forum district, Venus, the goddess of gardens and of vegetation, acquired a sanctuary (Venus Cloacina); and between it and the Comitium Janus, the god of entrances and exits, found his little temple,

FIG. 4. S. Pietro in Carcere, Oratorio del Crocefisso, S. Giuseppe dei Falegnami

the doors of which later remained open whenever a war was in progress.

Between these two groups of buildings, below the Capitol and the Palatine, lay the open market place to which the citizens came from their city homes and the peasants from the Campagna, bringing such things as they wished to sell, and so the old Roman scholars explained the derivation of the word Forum as coming from *ferre* to bring or carry, incorrectly of course. This open space served also for processions and for celebrations, and especially for the funeral games at the burial of patricians. The two long sides of the market place were occupied by stalls or booths (*tabernae*), originally simple wooden shacks where butchers and green grocers plied their trade.

From the beginning of the Republic on we hear of the erection of magnificent sanctuaries in the Forum: at the lower end of the Clivus Capitolinus the temple of Saturn, protector of the crops, was dedicated in 497 B.C.; at the opposite end, beside the shrine of Juturna, the temple of the Dioscuri (Templum Castorum) was dedicated in 484 B.C. Public life likewise began to drift from the Comitium to the Forum; magistrates sat in judgment at the upper end of the open space below the Capitol; and when in 450 B.C. Rome produced her first written law, the Twelve Tables on which the law was recorded were nailed to the old speakers' platform at the boundary of the Forum and the Comitium. After the close of the bitter strife between the patricians and the plebeians which largely fills up the first 150 years of the Republic, the temple of Concord (Templum Concordiae) was dedicated at the foot of the Capitol above the Comitium by Marcus Furius Camillus, the conqueror of the Gauls.

All the temples mentioned above originally had walls and columns made of native rock, just as it was shipped into the City from the neighboring quarries, brown or red tufa or grayish green peperino, for even the lovely limestone from Tivoli (lapis Tiburtinus or travertine) was not in use until later centuries. Walls and columns were faced with stucco, cornices and pediment revetments consisted of brightly painted terra cotta slabs, and the statues of the gods in the pediments and in the cellas were made of terra cotta. The best idea of this method of building may be obtained from the temples of southern Etruria and of Campania; the model of the temple of Alatri which was erected in the court of the Museo di Villa Giulia is particularly instructive. The life size terra cotta statue of Apollo from Veii, likewise in the Museo di Villa Giulia, offers the best example of the type of temple statues.

The settlement of the struggle between the classes at home and the victory over mighty opponents such as the Etruscans and the Samnites considerably enlarged and strengthened the power and the wealth of the Roman state in the fourth century B.C., and this development naturally had its influence also on the capital. The numerous structural improvements and embellishments which the Forum underwent at this period are associated especially with the name of C. Maenius. As consul he conquered the people of Antium in 338 B.C. and he decorated the speakers' platform with the beaks of the war ships he captured, whereupon it received the name of Rostra; twenty years later, as censor, he removed the stalls of the butchers and the green grocers from the Forum—a food market, *macellum,* was built especially for them north of the Forum—and restored the booths in which thereafter money changers and bankers were accommodated (tabernae argentariae). The two rows of shops, called *veteres* on the north side and *novae* on the south, were probably identical in appearance: they were one story high and had a flat roof with a gallery from which it was possible to watch the games in the Forum; the name maeniana which was still in use during the Empire to designate the tiers of seats in the Roman theatres and amphitheatres commemorated the man who introduced this custom.

An honorary column (Columna Maenia) was erected to Maenius in recognition of his services, at the boundary of the Forum and the Comitium. No trace of this column remains, but we still possess a fragment of the base of another honorary column (Columna Rostrata) with the honorary inscription upon it which was dedicated to the Consul C. Duilius to celebrate his naval victory over Carthage. This is, however, only a marble copy of the original and dates from the early Empire (now in the Capitoline Museum). It became the custom at this time and later to erect statues of deserving citizens in the Forum or near the Forum, but the number of them gradually grew so great that even in 158 B.C. the censors ordered the removal of all the statues which had not been erected by the Senate and the People.

In the second century B.C. the intercourse of Rome with Greece and with the Hellenistic East became livelier. Among other things the Romans borrowed from those old civilizations the design for the great public porticoes, the basilicas, which thereafter were regarded as necessary adjuncts of any forum. These Roman basilicas were not intended for religious uses as were the later Christian basilicas developed from them, but for practical purposes, such as markets or law courts. They were spacious structures, most of them with three or five aisles supported on columns or piers with the light streaming in through the raised central nave. The first basilica in Rome was built in 185 B.C. by the Censor M. Porcius Cato, west of the Comitium near the Carcer, but every trace of it has disappeared. Of the second basilica, however, there are considerable remains, though only in reconstruction dating from imperial times. This hall, the Basilica Aemilia, was erected by the censors for the year 179 B.C., M. Fulvius Nobilior and M. Aemilius Lepidus, on the north side of the Forum behind the so-called old shops; a third basilica, erected by Tiberius Sempronius Gracchus in 170 B.C. at the Vicus Tuscus west of the temple of Castor, was sacrificed in building the Basilica Julia.

About the middle of the second century B.C., the enormously increased political activity at Rome made the old Comitium seem too small for the popular assembly and in 145 the meetings were transferred to the Forum. In the decades following, especially in the time of the Gracchi, the Forum thus often became the scene of embittered party strife. We also hear of various monuments at this period intended as embellishments for the Forum, such as the honorary arch of the Fabii at the east end of the Forum, spanning the entrance to the Sacra Via; and also of new buildings, among others a fourth basilica beside the temple of Concord (Basilica Opimia, 121 B.C.).

In the Civil Wars between Marius and Sulla, the Capitol, and probably also the Forum, suffered serious damage. Then when Sulla reached the dictatorship he conceived extensive plans for reconstruction. Of the buildings executed at his order the only one that has been preserved is the Tabularium (Public Record Office) between the two peaks of the Capitoline Hill, which long formed an imposing perspective for the Forum.

Of the remaining activity of Sulla and his assistants, which must have been very extensive, there are merely insignificant traces in many spots under the imperial level which have only recently been properly observed and correctly interpreted.

The great reorganization which gave the Forum the shape which it retained throughout imperial times was the work of Caesar the Dictator. He transferred the popular assembly from the Forum, which was in turn growing too small for it, out to the Campus Martius; the old Comitium was to a great extent built over by a new Senate house (Curia Julia); on the south side of the area, corresponding to the Basilica Aemilia, arose a second magnificent portico, the Basilica Julia. The new speakers' platform

(Rostra Julia) was transferred to the west side of the Forum, and opposite it the dictator himself soon after acquired a temple (Templum Divi Julii). This is the Forum begun by Caesar, completed by Augustus and embellished repeatedly by later emperors, which the excavations have presented to our view.

THE FORUM IN IMPERIAL TIMES

THE ruins of the Forum as presented in the two views in plates 4 and 5 from the east (the Velia) and from the west (the Capitol) go back for the most part to the earlier centuries of the Empire and allow us to visualize the appearance of the Forum about the time of Trajan and of Hadrian. In reconstructing these epochs we must eliminate some monuments which are now especially conspicuous, such as the triumphal arch of Septimius Severus (203 A.D.); the huge columns on brick bases on the south side of the Forum opposite the front elevation of the Basilica Julia (fourth century A.D.) and the column of Phocas (608 A.D.).

The Forum was an important knot in the net work of the city streets: The Sacra Via, ostensibly the oldest of all, descended from the Velia (at the arch of Titus), debouched in the Forum between the temple of Faustina and the temple of Caesar and continued along on the west side of the area of the Forum, as the Clivus Capitolinus, which led to the temple of Jupiter Capitolinus. From the Tiber and the Forum Boarium through the valley of the Velabrum ran the Vicus Tuscus below the Palatine, and the Vicus Jugarius at the slope of the Capitol. They entered the Forum at the Basilica Julia, the former at the east side, the latter at the west. Vicus Jugarius is erroneously translated by the moderns as Yoke Makers' Street, but as ancient authors tell us, it was probably named after an altar to Juno Juga.

On the north side the broad Argiletum ran along beside the Curia (S. Adriano) to the Esquiline; later the greater part of it was included in the Forum of Nerva. Still another street led westward from the Comitium and the Carcer to the Campus Martius. In ancient times this was probably called Lautumiae (Quarry Lane); the name frequently used instead, Clivus Argentarius, is mediaeval.

In the following description we shall start at the east side of the open area of the Forum with the temple of Caesar, proceed to the south side (Basilica Julia), then to the west side (the temples at the Clivus Capitolinus, the arch of Severus, the Comitium and the Rostra) and finally to the north side (Basilica Aemilia). Then leaving the Forum proper we come to the temple of Castor and the sanctuary of Juturna, the temple of Augustus with its library and the Christian church built into it (S. Maria Antiqua), the temple of Vesta and the House of the Vestals and finally the Sacra Via as far as the arch of Titus and the temple of Venus and Rome.

FIG. 5. Temple of Caesar

The temple of the Deified Caesar (Templum Divi Julii) was erected on the spot where the body of the Dictator was burned on March 15, 44 B.C. It was dedicated by Augustus on August 18, 29 B.C. In addition to what we learn from the remains unearthed by the excavations we get our idea of its appearance from representations on coins (Fig. 5). The temple rose on a high substructure; it had a roomy portico with six columns at the front and a comparatively small cella, as it was wider than deep. Then instead of having a broad flight of steps leading up to the portico there were only two narrow staircases at the sides in consequence of the peculiar construction of the façade. In front, in the centre of the substructure, is a large semi-circular niche (plate 6), in which is preserved the base of what appears to be a round altar. The two straight walls at either side of the niche were ornamented, as the representations on coins show, with the beaks of ships in two rows, one above the other; these were the trophies from Cleopatra's fleet which Augustus took at Actium. The Rostra ad Divi Julii is seldom mentioned, and it seems to have been used especially for funeral orations for members of the imperial family.

The temple survived the fall of paganism; indeed the wall of grayish green tufa blocks carelessly piled up which now closes the niche probably dates from Christian times, when it was considered desirable to preserve the monument which commemorated the Founder of the Empire, but at the same time necessary to make it impossible to perform pagan rites and sacrifices at the altar. The temple of Caesar was flanked by two honorary arches, the (older) arch of the Fabii (see below, p. 35) at the north and the arch of Augustus at the south. The foundations of the latter, a handsome monument with three passages, were lately uncovered. It was erected in 19 B.C. by the Senate and the People on the occasion of the recovery of the Roman standards which had been lost in the Parthian war in 55 B.C. Its appearance is known to us (Fig. 6) from representations on coins and it is very probable that the fragments of Doric columns, capitals and entablatures of extremely fine workmanship found near it and formerly thought to be a part of the decoration of the Regia (see below, p. 36 f.) belonged to the decoration of the side passages of the arch.

Only a few steps from the temple of Caesar and the arch of Augustus we find another monument to the Founder of the Empire, the Basilica Julia, which occupies the south side of the Forum (plate 7). It was planned by Caesar before the Gallic War was over (54 B.C.) and dedicated by him eight years later (Sept. 26, 46 B.C.) in an unfinished condition. It received its final form under Augustus after being damaged by fire and was dedicated for the second time by the emperor in 12 A.D. The building was frequently restored, even in later times (the beginning of the fifth century, A.D.), and survived the fall of the Empire. In the eighth or ninth century a little Christian church crept into the west portico on the ancient level. The name of this church is not known; it is generally called S. Maria in Cannapara, but this name really belongs to the little chapel of S. Maria delle Grazie, incorporated in the hospital della Consolazione. It is likewise an error to assume that the name Cannapara, which is arbitrarily translated rope-walk, belonged to the basilica in the early Middle Ages, while as a matter of fact it included the greater part of the older valley of the Velabrum.

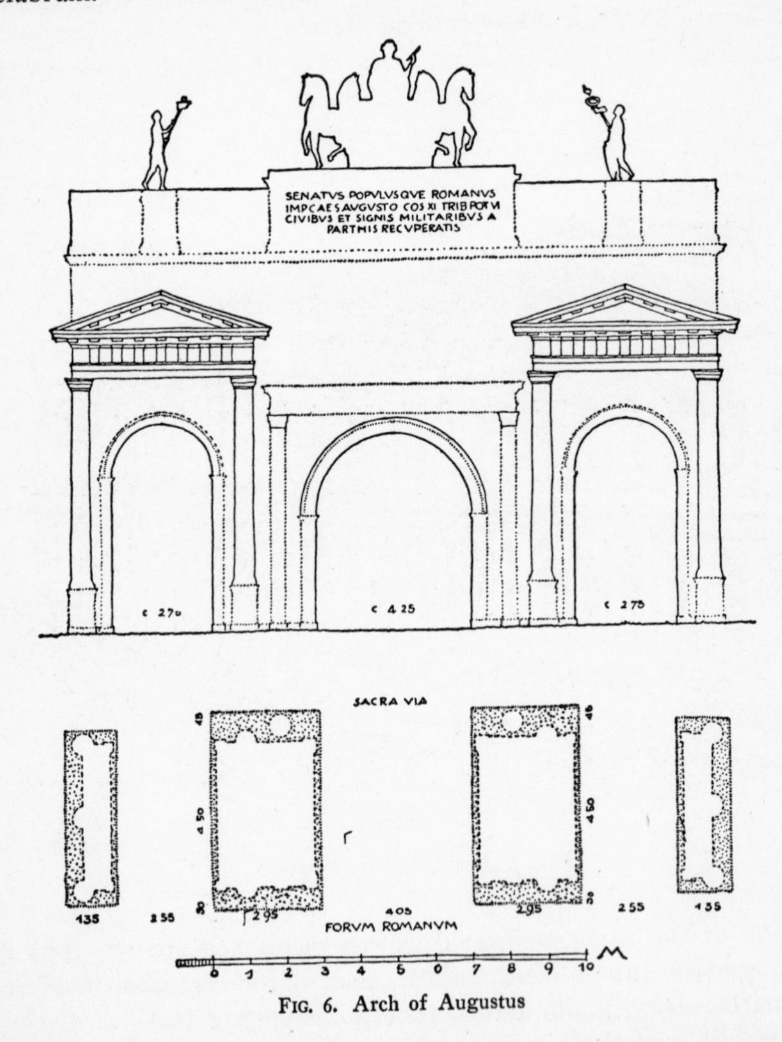

FIG. 6. Arch of Augustus

We enter the basilica (Fig. 7) from the side on the Vicus Tuscus by ten to twelve steps, while at the other side, on the Vicus Jugarius, the entrance portico lies almost exactly at the street level. The building consisted of one central hall surrounded by two two-storied porticoes.

The northern portico opened on the Forum with sixteen arcades while the central colonnade had twelve arcades on the long axes and three on the short sides. The façade on the Forum (plate 8) had pillars of solid marble with engaged columns projecting, while the pillars of the inner porticoes consisted of brick masonry with marble facing. The west portico, facing towards the Vicus Jugarius, is the best preserved, thanks to the in-

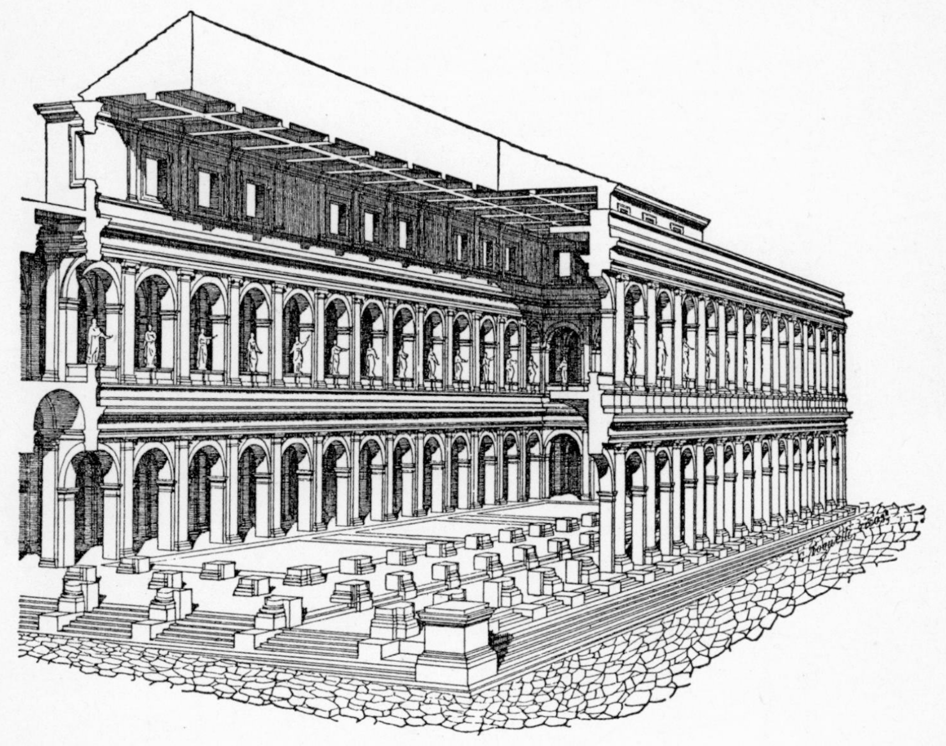

FIG. 7. Basilica Julia, restored

corporation of the early mediaeval church mentioned above. The floor of the side aisles was of white marble, that of the central hall, of costly colored marble slabs (giallo antico, africano, pavonazzetto).

The meetings of the Centumviral Court were held in the central hall, and each of the four divisions which constituted the court had its own magisterial tribunal for administering justice, but none of these wooden structures remains. The best preserved remains of the rear portico can still be seen at the southwest corner; walls of great tufa blocks built up to the pillars at the south side, probably to provide rooms for business or offices (scholae).

The street in front of the basilica was embellished early in the fourth century A.D. by the erection of seven enormous columns on pedestals made of cube-shaped bricks (see plates 7 and 8), which bear stamps of the time of Diocletian. It is conjectured that this ostentatious row of columns was erected to hide the damage done by a conflagration under the Emperor Carinus (283-284).

At the northwest corner of the basilica, not spanning the Sacra Via but beside it, stood a triumphal arch dating from early imperial times, corresponding to the arch of Augustus at the other end. And just as the latter celebrated the recovery of the military standards captured by the Parthians, so the former marked the occasion when the standards which were lost by Varus and his legions were recovered in the campaigns of Germanicus (14-16 A.D.). The foundations of this arch of Tiberius were uncovered in 1900 (see Fig. 8); architectural remains had been found earlier (1835, 1848); a portion of the attic which bears the beginning of the inscription SENATUS POPULUSQUE (Romanus) lies with other fragments near the last brick base.

Upon meeting the Vicus Jugarius the Sacra Via becomes the Clivus Capitolinus, as we mentioned above. At this point, behind the foundations of the arch of Augustus, we see a supporting wall, eight low arches of tufa blocks with spandrels of excellent reticulate work. It was probably constructed when it became necessary to move the street forward several metres toward the Forum when the temple of Saturn was reconstructed (by Munatius Plancus in 42 B.C.). There is no authority for calling this structure Rostra Caesaris or Rostra Vetera.

Close at hand, at the left of the Clivus stood the Golden Milestone (Milliarium Aureum), erected by Augustus in 10 B.C. This was a marble column covered with gilt-bronze on which the distances from Rome to the most important cities of Italy and of the Empire were engraved. Fragments of the marble column (with rough surfaces) and a richly decorated entablature belonging to it which were found here in 1835 are now lying at the foot of the Clivus.

Over the Vicus Jugarius and the Clivus Capitolinus rises the imposing temple of Saturn, one of the best preserved of all those in the Forum (plate 9). It was founded in the early days of the Republic (497 B.C.; see above, p. 9), but owes its present form for the most part to a reconstruction by L. Munatius Plancus (42 B.C.). To the latter are also probably due the magnificent substructures of travertine blocks on the side towards the

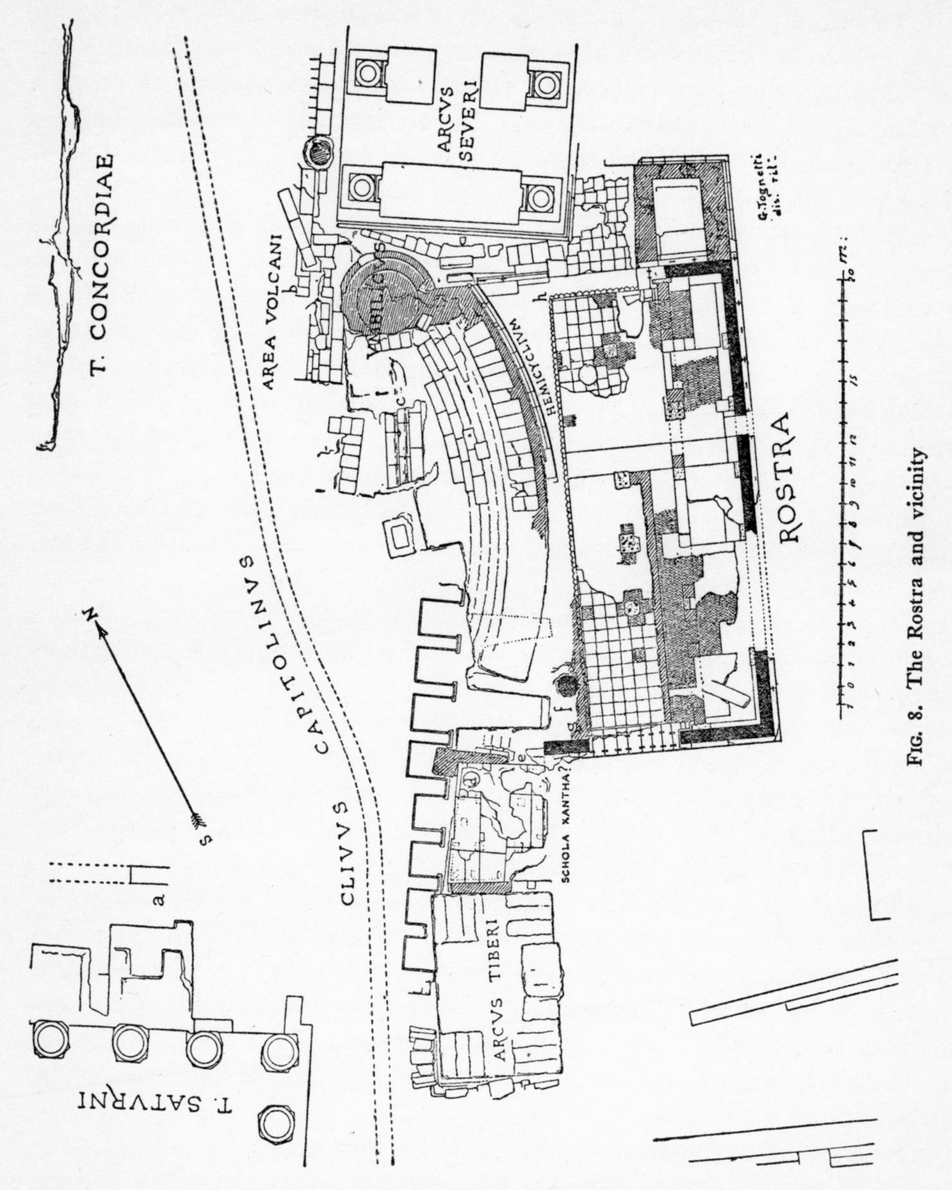

FIG. 8. The Rostra and vicinity

Vicus Jugarius. The rooms in the substructure served a practical purpose, namely the safeguarding of the state treasure (Aerarium Saturni), and as a result the building was preserved even after the fall of paganism. The portico with its eight unfluted columns of gray and of red granite was restored at a late date after a fire, as the inscription proves: *Senatus populusque Romanus incendio consumptum restituit.* It is worthy of note that the name of no god is mentioned. The work on the bases and the capitals of the columns is careless and uneven; the inner side of the architrave, which is easily visible from the steps of the Capitol, consists for the most part of beautifully decorated blocks which were taken from the Forum of Trajan and to which the rough workmanship of the restored portions forms a distinct contrast. That the Forum of Trajan was plundered in the fourth century A.D. for the decoration of newly erected buildings is attested by the triumphal arch of Constantine, and the restoration of the temple of Saturn also probably belongs to Christian times, the fourth century at the earliest.

Behind the temple of Saturn lies a terrace resting on a foundation composed of seven chambers of good brick work, which at the rear abuts on the front of the Tabularium and the substructures of the Clivus Capitolinus (plate 10). The obtuse angle formed by these two lines is filled in by a portico having columns of green veined cipollino with travertine capitals bearing military trophies. The inscription on the entablature proves that the city prefect Vettius Agorius Praetextatus in 367 A.D. either arranged or restored the statues of the twelve Olympian deities and the entire decoration of the area. Even in the time of Caesar there were statues of the twelve gods in the Forum; the building of Praetextatus, the last monument of paganism in the Forum, was undoubtedly constructed from architectural parts of older buildings. The portico was excavated in 1834 and greatly restored in 1858.

In front of the façade of the Tabularium, between it and the Clivus, stand three lovely Corinthian columns with entablature in place (see plate 9). These belong to the temple which Domitian dedicated to his father Vespasian and to his brother Titus in 81 A.D. The inscription on the façade, of which today only the last letters of the last word are preserved, was still in a complete state of preservation in the time of Charlemagne, and was copied at that time. It attested the dedication by Domitian and a restoration by Severus and Caracalla (193–211 A.D.). The front elevation of the temple (together with the façade of the Tabularium behind it) is shown in the reconstruction on plate 11. On the frieze are sculptured sacrificial implements and skulls of oxen. The very fine work on the reliefs can be judged even better from the casts in the Tabularium (plate 12, right) which were restored with the help of ancient fragments, than from the originals. The walls of the cella are in ruins with the exception of a few fragments. In the centre of the rear wall which leans against the Tabularium is still preserved the pedestal for the statues of the two deified emperors.

North of the temple of Vespasian and likewise leaning against the Tabularium lie the foundations of a large temple, the name of which we owe to the same pilgrim of the time of Charlemagne who copied the inscription from the temple of Vespasian. He saw the façade of the third temple still in place and on it the inscription according to which the Senate and the Roman People restored the temple of Concordia. This temple of the goddess of Concord was founded, as we mentioned above, by Marcus Furius Camillus in 366 B.C., but the original building has completely disappeared as well as the reconstruction by L. Opimius (121 B.C.). The remains which were for the most part brought to light by the excavations of 1811 belong to the magnificent reconstruction by Tiberius (7 B.C. to 10 A.D.). In this reconstruction the cella of the temple received an unusual form, being almost twice as wide as deep. Marble pedestals which were discovered here in 1817 prove that it contained statues of noble metals (5 pounds of gold and 25 pounds of silver); furthermore, as we learn from literary evidence, many valuable works of art by Greek masters were kept in the temple. In the Tabularium (plate 12, left) may be seen a cleverly restored cast of the charming principal entablature of the structure of Tiberius.

The temples at the Clivus with the magnificently plain façade of the Tabularium rising in the background formed the monumental western boundary of the Forum in the first two centuries of the Christian era, but this impression was to a great extent destroyed when in 203 A.D. the large triple arch was erected in honor of the emperor, Septimius Severus (plate 13), which is today one of the most conspicuous monuments in the whole Forum.

The occasion was the campaigns of the emperor and his sons against the Parthians and the Arabs in the country lying between the Euphrates and the Tigris (193, 198, 199 A.D.). After the campaigns were over, Severus returned to Rome in 203 A.D., and celebrated the tenth anniversary of his reign, without however enjoying a triumph; in the same year the arch was erected by the Senate and the People to honor him and his two sons. On the inscription we can still read, after the name of Severus, that of his elder son, Antoninus (Caracalla); and while the name of the younger brother Geta formerly stood in the line following (the fourth), it was erased, as it was from all monuments, after Caracalla got rid of his brother and colleague by murder in the year 212. In place of Geta's name we find on the stone new laudatory epithets for Severus and Caracalla. The reliefs portray in greater detail than on other arches the military acts of the three rulers: On the face towards the Capitol at the upper right-hand corner we have the beginning of the campaign, the formal address (allocutio) of the emperor to his troops; next, lower down, on the right and on the left, are shown the storming of a beleaguered town with the battering ram, a cavalry engagement and other battles. The reliefs on the face toward the Forum are similar in character, but are less well preserved. The influence of the reliefs of the columns of Trajan and Antoninus is evident, but so also is the rapid deterioration of Roman art in the course of one generation. In the spandrels over the central arch may be seen Victories bearing trophies, and, below, the genii of the four seasons. The arch served as a pedestal for the imperial statues, as according to representations on coins Severus was shown with his sons in a six horse chariot.

Beside the arch of Severus and to the left (south, see Fig. 8) is a conical monument of brick work with three steps which was originally faced with marble: the Umbilicus Urbis Romae, the imaginary centre of the city which symmetrically balanced the Milliarium Aureum (see above, p. 18). The erection of this monument is perhaps connected with the reconstruction of the Rostra occasioned by the building of the arch of Severus (see below, p. 23). Remains of very ancient tufa foundations between the Umbilicus and the temple of Concord are supposed to have belonged to a sanctuary of Vulcan (Volcanal, see above, p. 2), founded by Romulus, according to the legend, and still standing in the time of Augustus; and the pits in the native tufa near-by possibly go back to an archaic cemetery (see above, p. 2).

Near the Volcanal Romulus is supposed to have arranged the first place for speeches to the populace, as suggested by several of the Roman scholars, and perhaps this tradition was not without influence on the choice of the spot to which Augustus moved his new speakers' platform, according to ancient testimony, at the boundary of the Comitium and the Forum (see below, p. 29). The speakers' platform of Augustus was a handsome structure, stretching across nearly the whole of the west side of the Forum; about 24 metres (80 Roman feet) wide and 4 metres high. In the tufa blocks of the front wall can still be seen the pairs of holes which served to fasten the ships' beaks (rostra) which ornamented this structure. The tufa wall was originally faced with marble and had a projecting marble base and cornice of which fragments have been found (plate 14). The platform was a rectangle 24 by 10 metres, and intended not for a single speaker but for the emperor and his retinue (cf. the reproduction on the reliefs from the balustrade, plate 15). It was approached from the rear from the Clivus Capitolinus by a flight of six steps set in a slight curve (Fig. 9). In front and at each side the platform was fenced in with a

FIG. 9. The platform of the Rostra, from the rear

marble balustrade, and marble reliefs were set into the centre of the lateral balustrades after the time of Trajan (see p. 24, f.).

At a later date, perhaps at the time when the arch of Severus was built, the platform was cut up by the building in of a little court of irregular plan (Fig. 10). The rear wall of it followed the outline of the curved steps; the facing of decorative colored and white marble is still well preserved and stone masons' marks (Greek letters) on the lower moulding show that it never extended beyond the central axis of the platform. A structure so unsymmetrical as this cannot, as has been asserted, be older than the Augustan Rostra which stands in front of it. At the right end of the curved wall towards the arch of Severus, it joins the Umbilicus Urbis

Romae, which is perhaps contemporary with it (see above, p. 22). At a very late date the façade was lengthened at the north end by an additional structure extremely careless in execution, which was likewise ornamented with the beaks of ships; it has been suggested that it was erected on the occasion of a naval victory over the Vandals about 470 A.D.

The two large balustrades beautifully decorated on both sides with charming reliefs which were found a short distance from the Rostra in 1872, were a part of the decoration of it (plate 15 and Fig. 11, "Anaglypha"). At the time of excavation they were found quite roughly set on the travertine sills which still serve as foundations for them, though the marble socle which has been shoved in between the balustrades and the sills is modern. They were thus set up twice on the same spot where they

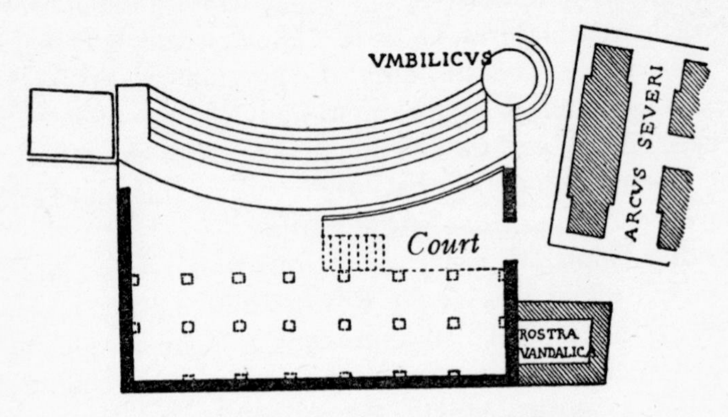

FIG. 10. Later Reconstruction of the Rostra

still stand today, probably indeed as the sides of a rectangular base, intended like the brick bases on the Sacra Via to support a monument, perhaps in honor of an emperor of a much later date. The two shorter sides of this rectangle, now in ruins, were closed up with brick work, and the space within filled with rubbish and mortar. Thus the surfaces of the slabs facing inward, which bear the sacrificial animals, were protected, while the outer surfaces, with the historical scenes were exposed for centuries to injury of every kind from the weather or the hand of man. This explains the remarkable difference in the state of preservation of the two surfaces. Regarding the period of this second utilization it is possible only to hazard a conjecture and we may conclude that it was in Christian times and after the time of Constantine, since the representation of the heathen sacrifice was covered over, while the historical scenes were allowed to remain visible.

The original location of the balustrades is indicated by the reliefs themselves for on both the monuments of the Forum form the background and in the foreground the Rostra, identified by the decoration of ships' beaks, is repeated at a significant point in the historical scenes. Again, their position in the centre of the balustrades at either side of the platform explains the difference in scale of the reliefs on the two faces of the slabs, for while the observer on the platform had the historical scenes directly before him, the sacrificial animals were visible only at a distance of about five metres.

On the balustrade which is incomplete (the last block on the right is wanting), we see at the extreme right (plate 15, 1) a hexastyle Ionic temple, to the left of it a hexastyle Corinthian temple, and between the two, at the level of the entablatures, an arch. The first temple is that of Saturn, the second Vespasian's and the arch a suggestion of the façade of the Tabularium. On the block at the right, now lost, the temple of Concord must have been shown, and the portico to the left of the temple of Saturn indicates the Basilica Julia. We have therefore on this relief a representation of the west and south sides of the Forum.

On the other balustrade, which is entirely preserved (plate 15, 2) we see behind the representation of the Rostra an arch (now replaced by the arch of Severus) a templelike structure with a flight of steps at the front (the Curia of Caesar), a broad street (the Argiletum, leading to the Forum of Nerva) and a portico exactly corresponding to that on the other balustrade (the Basilica Aemilia). At the extreme end of each relief we see the statue of a satyr (Marsyas) carrying a wine skin on his back and beside him a fig tree with a balustrade around it. These monuments were situated near the Tribunal Praetorium opposite the Rostra (see below, p. 27). The east end of the Forum opposite the speakers' platform which the orator saw before him as he stood on the platform is not shown. On the balustrade of the Rostra at the right of the speaker was the relief with the representation of the west and south sides of the area, and on his left the one showing the north side. The animals of the expiatory sacrifice, which were seen on the outer side as if in solemn procession (plate 15, 3), were perhaps intended to commemorate a ceremony such as took place at the establishment of the Rostra or at a reconstruction of it under Trajan.

The historical scenes which are pictured as taking place in front of this background, i.e., in the middle of the Forum, do honor to the Emperor

Trajan (98-117 A.D.) as the benefactor of Italy and the provinces, in suggestive form: on the balustrade which now faces the arch of Severus, the one that is entirely preserved (plate 15, 2), the emperor stands with his retinue on the Rostra and makes an announcement which is received with acclamation by his auditors. The audience is composed of the populace, recognizable as such by their dress, which is not the voluminous toga but

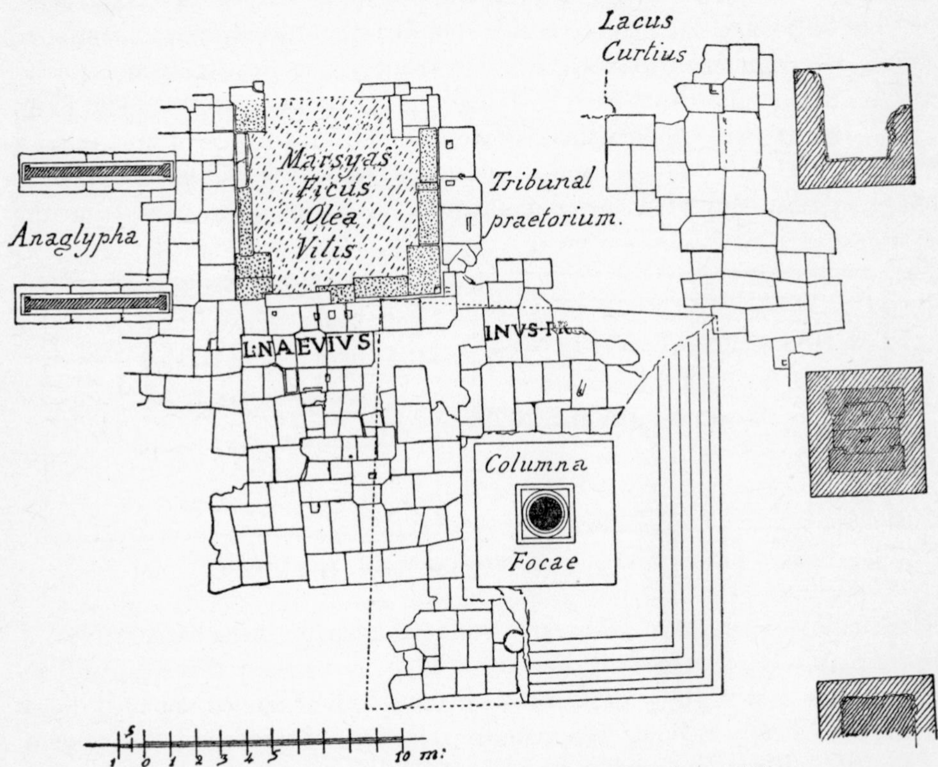

FIG. 11. Balustrades of Trajan, Praetorian Tribunal, Column of Phocas

the short plebeian garment, the paenula. The subject of the imperial address was indicated by the sculptor in a way which every one of his contemporaries would recognize, that is, by placing in the midst of the auditors a sculptured group as it probably stood in the Forum in his day. The group shows the emperor seated on a curule chair, and being approached by a woman who carries one child and leads another by the hand. This same figure with the two children appears also on coins of Trajan which were struck to commemorate a magnificent charitable foundation of his for the feeding and education of poor children, Institutio Alimentaria. The grateful woman is Italia, for the charity was limited to the mother country of the Empire.

On the other relief (plate 15, 1) the emperor, seated on the Rostra, gives the order to burn documents or legal papers (diptycha) which are being brought up by officials in military dress. This celebrates a great tax remission by which Trajan relieved the provinces—Italy was tax free.

The satyr and the fig tree beside him are reminiscent, as we mentioned above, of a significant spot which lay in front of the Rostra, symmetrically with its façade, the Praetorian Tribunal, the birthplace of Roman law (Fig. 11). It was here that the magistrates handed down their decisions on a tribunal originally only of wood. Beside it stood the statue of the satyr Marsyas as a sign of its penal judicature, a symbol taken over from the

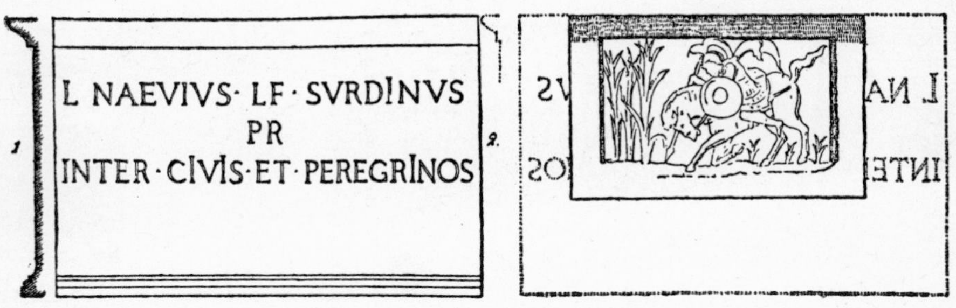

FIG. 12. Inscription and Relief from the Lacus Curtius

Greek cities of southern Italy, and beside the statue three sacred trees, a fig tree, an olive tree and a grapevine. The site of these three can still be identified as it is the only spot in the Forum which remained unpaved down to the late Empire, lying between the reliefs of Trajan and the column of Phocas. It was not until a very late date that it was roughly paved with bits of marble and fragments of inscriptions. Close by on the slabs of travertine of the old pavement dating from the time of Augustus, we see the beginning of an inscription in large letters originally picked out in metal, running from north to south, parallel with the façade of the Rostra. It proves that a praetor by the name of L. Naevius Surdinus, who probably held office under Tiberius, erected or restored a monument on this spot. Now the name of Surdinus appears also on a large marble bas-relief which was excavated in the year 1553 at the same spot in a garden near the column of Phocas, and is now preserved in the Palazzo dei Conservatori (Fig.

12). It probably belongs to the rear wall of the Tribunal restored by Surdinus; as for the rest, no trace remains of the structure, which was mostly of wood, even during the Empire.

The marble slab with the Surdinus inscription bears on the other side a relief in archaic style of a horseman plunging into a swampy abyss. According to an ancient Roman legend, in the war between the Romans and the Sabines after the rape of their women a Sabine leader, Mettius Curtius, stumbled into a swamp in the Forum, which was named Lacus Curtius after him. Later this form of the legend gave way to another according to which a noble youth, Marcus Curtius, rescued the city from destruction by hurling himself into a fiery gulf which yawned in the Forum. The so-called Lacus Curtius was, as late as the Empire, a dry well head enclosed by a marble

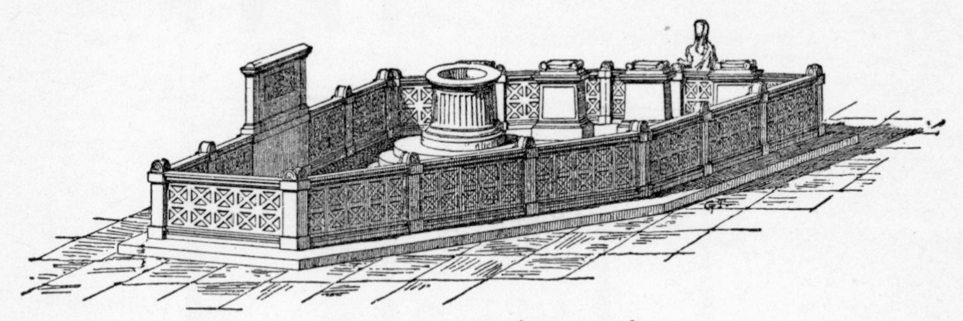

FIG. 13. Lacus Curtius, restored

lattice fence (Fig. 13). The remains of the sanctuary were brought to light in the excavations of 1904.

In front of the façade of the Rostra, facing on the Sacra Via, rises a column on a marble pedestal, set high on a brick base (plate 16). Never overturned itself, it was for centuries a reminder of the buried Forum, and actively stimulated the imagination of scholars. Many called it Columna Maenia, others thought it a fragment of the bridge which Caligula threw over the Palatine to the temple of Jupiter Capitolinus. But when in 1811 the rubbish was removed from the marble pedestal, the inscription was brought to light according to which the Byzantine exarch Smaragdus in 608 A.D. set up on the column a statue of Phocas, the reigning emperor of that time (602-610). The monument on which Smaragdus placed his inscription is however undoubtedly older; the brick base goes back probably to the fourth century A.D., the column and the capital are still older, dating from the second century and had been used once before they were erected on the brick base. An addition from Phocas' day may be the terraced pyramid which was constructed by using the wreckage from monuments in the vicinity, and which partly covered up the site of the Praetorian Tribunal. It has lately been cleared on the north and east sides.

We turn now to the north side of the Forum where, in the vicinity of the arch of Severus, it joins the smaller area of the Comitium, originally intended for the gathering of the people. The older Rostra stood at the

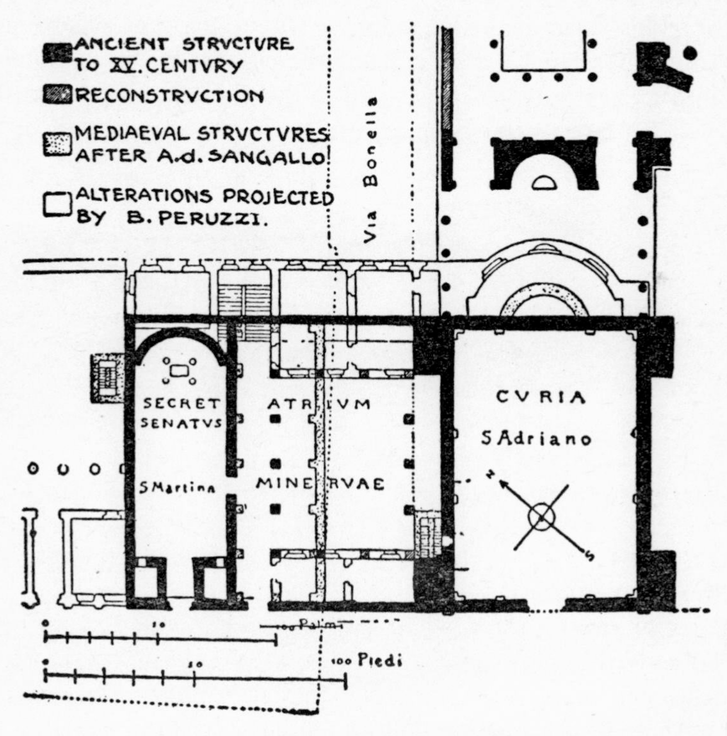

FIG. 14. Plan of the Curia Julia

junction of the Forum and the Comitium, near the grave of Romulus. The remains of tufa walls which were found under the imperial level between the grave of Romulus and the façade of the church of S. Adriano are assigned to this earlier speakers' platform. These walls run exactly from east to west, at right angles to the façade of the Carcer; and this agrees with the position of the Comitium, which was a square oriented to the four cardinal points of the compass. The length of each side can be estimated at about ninety metres or three hundred Roman feet. Only a small portion of this space is cleared today. As early as 50 B.C. a considerable portion was built over, when the Dictator Caesar established a new large Senate House, the Curia Julia, to replace the old Curia Hostilia, supposed to have been founded by the third king, Tullus Hostilius. The plan of the Curia Julia is still preserved (Fig. 14); only of course the building is in the form it received in later reconstructions, especially under Diocletian (303 A.D.). The Curia Julia was, as represented on coins and on the Rostra reliefs, a structure with a low portico and a high pediment. The inscription on the frieze beginning IMP. CAESAR called attention to the fact that it was Augustus who completed the building. Between the frieze and the roof of the portico three large windows admitted light to the interior. Besides the large assembly room the building contained also a smaller hall for secret or committee meetings (Secretarium Senatus), and several adjoining rooms. It was fortunate for the preservation of these buildings that they were transformed into Christian churches so early. The large hall was dedicated by Pope Honorius I (625-638) to the martyr Hadrianus of Nicomedia and the Secretarium probably not much later to the martyred Roman virgin, Martina. The façade of S. Adriano is essentially still that of Diocletian's Curia (Fig. 15), for it took over from the Curia of Caesar and Augustus the pediment and the three tall windows, now walled up, while the portico was not restored. The large brick wall which is now bare of ornament was covered with stucco to imitate marble facing. The façade of S. Adriano is a good place to observe the gradual elevation of level which occurred in the Middle Ages (plate 17); for the entrance portal was twice raised so that the sill of the modern door lies at the height of the lintel of the Diocletian door, and the ancient doorway was likewise twice walled up, the lower half with fragments of marble, porphyry and other valuable building stones, the upper portion with rough blocks of tufa. The first rise, which lies about three metres above the level of Diocletian's building, was perhaps connected in some way with a restoration of the church under Gregory IX (1229); in the centuries which followed, the ground rose again considerably so that, as is shown in old drawings and engravings, by the end of the 16th century it was necessary to descend steps to the entrance. When in 1654 the church was again restored the door was once again raised about three metres, and as a consequence it became necessary to block the ancient windows. The modern church of S. Martina, commonly called S. Martina e Luca, is likewise a full story above the original church, which now serves as a crypt. Until the lower church was rebuilt by Pietro da Cortona (about 1640) its apse was preserved with an inscription according to which the prefect of the City, Flavius Annius Eucharius Epiphanius, in 412 A.D. restored the Secretarium, which had been seriously damaged in the attack of the Goths under

FIG. 15. Façade of the Curia Julia, restored

Alaric. S. Martina and S. Adriano were in ancient times connected by a colonnade (Atrium Minervae) of which remains were still visible in the 16th century; the Via Bonella which now runs between the two churches was laid out only under Sixtus V (1585-1590).

East of the Curia and separated from it by an ancient street lies the Basilica Aemilia which during the Empire dominated the whole of the north side of the Forum (plate 18). This, the oldest of the original basilicas in the Forum (founded 179 B.C., see above, p. 11), is preserved essentially in the form which it received when it was rebuilt under Augustus and Tiberius. It consisted of three main parts, the portico, the single rooms (tabernae) and the main hall. The entrance portico was two stories high, the lower story in Doric style with a lovely frieze with triglyphs and metopes. A portion of the west side of the lower story stood, a magnificent ruin, opposite the side wall of S. Adriano till the end of the 15th century; a drawing which Giuliano da Sangallo made of the remains in 1480 is reproduced on plate 19, below. The remains were destroyed by Bramante in the construction of the palace of the Cardinal of Corneto (now Torlonia) at the Piazza Scossacavalli.

One did not, as in the Basilica Julia, pass directly into the main hall from the portico, but a row of square rooms separated from one another ran between the two; these tabernae or scholae undoubtedly served some practical purpose such as offices etc., like similar rooms in the Basilica Julia at the rear of the main hall.

The main hall was 29.5 metres wide (100 Roman feet), and more than 70 metres long, with an elevated central nave and one side aisle at the south side toward the Forum and two aisles on the north side. The porticoes, two stories in height (Fig. 16) had columns of costly colored marble, africano, and above, entablatures of white marble of the finest workmanship. On two fragments of the architrave we find remains of an inscription badly damaged by fire: PAVL . . RESTI . . . probably referring to the Consul Paullus Aemilius Lepidus, who restored the building twice under Augustus, in 34 and in 14 B.C.

The pavement of the central aisle consists of large slabs of colored marble (giallo, cipollino etc.). In many spots fragments of bronze and of iron are fused with the marble, obviously as the result of a fire which found ample food in the wooden ceilings of the side aisles and of the central aisle. A heap of coins likewise fused with the marble is of interest in establishing the date of this catastrophe, as they belong in the fourth century (post Constantine epoch), so far as it is possible to recognize their mintage. Probably the conflagration which damaged the Senate House (see above, p. 31) at the time of the Gothic invasion under Alaric in 410 A.D. reached the basilica also. When, later, the basilica was reconstructed as well as could be expected, the damaged pavement was not replaced with a new one at the same level, but a much coarser one was laid over the other at a slight elevation. Thus the marks of the fire and the fragments of metal and the coins were completely preserved.

At the southeast corner of the basilica near the temple of Faustina is a heap of great blocks of marble with an honorary inscription in very good lettering. It was set up by the Senate in the year 2 B.C. in honor of the adoptive son of Augustus, the young Lucius Caesar. There must have been a second one as well perhaps dedicated by the knights (Equites) to his brother Gaius; in all probability a third, dedicated to Augustus by the Plebs (Urbana), which was found near-by and had been built over in the Middle Ages, belongs

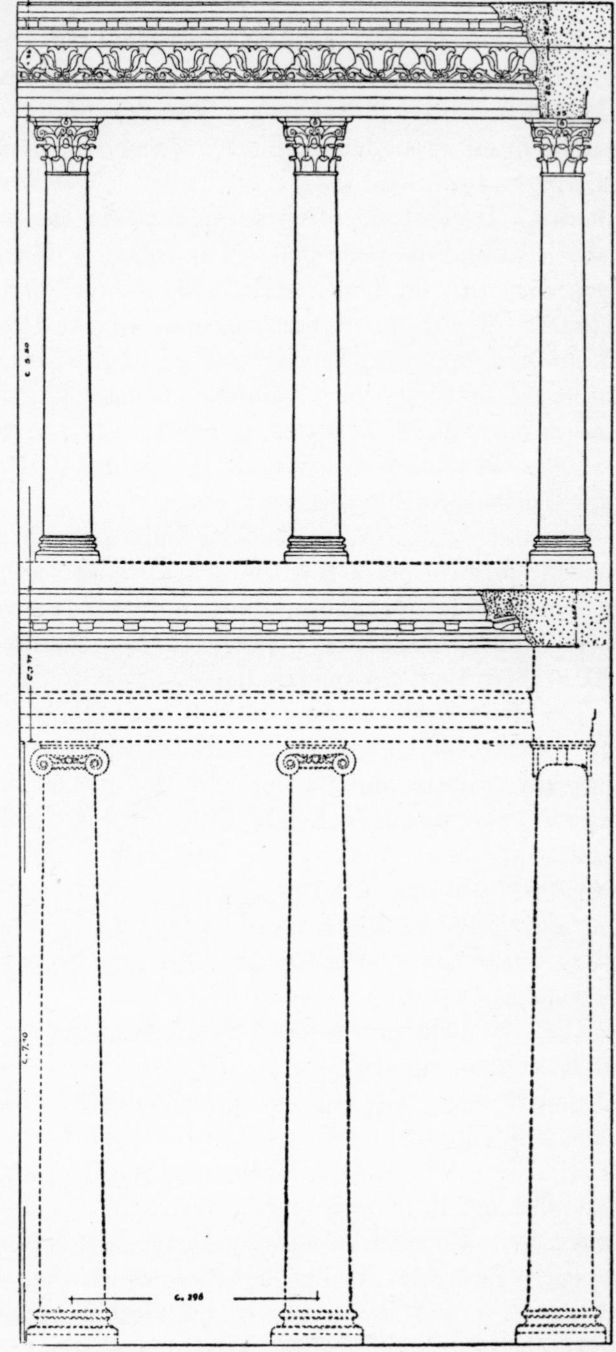

FIG. 16. Porticoes of the Main Room of the Basilica Aemilia

to the other two. All three of them were obviously structurally combined with the Basilica Aemilia; they were probably attached to the pavilionlike wing on the east hall of the basilica, towards the temple of Faustina, and it is probable that the east hall was called Porticus Julia after this monument to the imperial dynasty. A round well head, with a modern wall around it found in the east portico is probably correctly named Puteal Libonis (or Scribonianum), a sanctuary, perhaps a spot struck by lightning, which is often mentioned because judgments were pronounced at it. We are familiar with its appearance from coins and from a marble copy (Fig. 17).

We are still quite ignorant as to when the basilica fell completely into ruins. We find structures built into the east half of the so-called tabernae, dating from the seventh or eighth centuries (see plate 18), which were con-

FIG. 17. Puteal Libonis

structed by utilizing fragments from monuments in the vicinity, the Regia, among others. Probably the granite columns set on unwieldy cubical bases which are visible near the eastern corner are connected with these built-in structures.

In front of the basilica, near the west corner were situated two archaic sanctuaries, the temple of Janus and the shrine of Venus Cloacina. The first, of which no trace now remains, was a small square structure with two doors facing east and west respectively which were closed only when peace reigned over all the Roman world; the substructures of the second were brought to light by the recent excavations: a round base of travertine with marble moulding at the bottom and a stairway of only a few steps. On the upper surface surrounded by a fence, stood two female figures (Fig. 18), as is proved by representations on coins.

On the pavement of the area of the Forum can still be seen several additional remains of foundations of larger monuments. One such, in the centre of the area, between the Sacellum Cloacinae and the brick bases, is supposed to be the base of an equestrian statue of Constantine which was still visible in the centre of the Forum between the eighth and ninth centuries, although, judging from the construction, it is too poor for the time of Constantine. Next to it the foundations of a far larger monument were excavated under the pavement in 1903, the upper part of which had been purposely destroyed in ancient times. This foundation is ascribed with great probability to the colossal equestrian statue of Domitian, which was erected in his honor in the centre of the Forum. When, after the death of the emperor, the monuments to him were destroyed and his name erased wherever it occurred, this one also disappeared.

Under the pavement of the Forum of Caesar and Augustus runs a network of vaulted underground passages (cuniculi), which must have been constructed at the time the pavement was laid. The principal passage

FIG. 18. Sacellum Cloacinae

extends from the centre of the Rostra to the centre of the temple of Caesar; at right angles to this first one four crossroads run at intervals of about fifteen metres (50 Roman feet) with square vaulted chambers at either end. The purpose of this construction is not positively known, perhaps the chambers served in the setting up of machines by means of which heavy loads could be moved back and forth in the Forum without disturbing traffic.

The boundary of the Forum on the Sacra Via was supposed, in antiquity, to be the honorary arch of the Fabii. This was an ordinary arch made of travertine, erected in 121 B.C. by the Consul Quintus Fabius Maximus Allobrogicus and restored by his grandson and namesake probably in Caesar's day. Remains of the arch, notably the inscription, were excavated in the year 1546, but not preserved. According to the inscription the arch was decorated with the statues of L. Aemilius Paullus, the conqueror of Perseus of Macedon, Scipio Africanus the Younger and

Fabius Allobrogicus the Younger; and it is probable that statues of the elder Allobrogicus and the elder Scipio were likewise present. Even at the time of the excavations in 1882 blocks of the vaulting were found, incorporated in mediaeval structures. With great probability remains of a travertine foundation on the north side of the temple of Caesar have lately been identified as belonging to the arch.

Immediately behind the Fornix Fabianus on the left side of the Sacra Via lies the temple of Antoninus and Faustina, one of the best preserved monuments in the entire Forum (plate 20). This was originally dedicated to the empress alone by a decree of the Senate after her death, in 141, and her apotheosis, but after the emperor's death in 161 it was dedicated to him also. A broad flight of steps on which a large sacrificial altar can be recognized half way up, led to the portico whose ten columns of Euboean marble (cipollino) are unfluted. The cella walls are of peperino, and of the marble facing the frieze on the west wall, showing griffins grouped in pairs around a candelabrum is well preserved. The preservation of the building is due to the circumstance that as early as the 12th century a church, S. Lorenzo in Miranda, was built into it; the name Miranda is perhaps reminiscent of its founder.

Opposite the temple of Faustina and behind the temple of Caesar the foundations of a building of an irregular and complicated plan were discovered, which was recognized as the Regia, the official residence of the Pontifex Maximus (plate 21). In historical times it served not as a dwelling for the high priest, but as a religious arsenal and repository for the pontifical archives. Thus in one of the shrines dedicated to Mars, the sacred spears of the god were kept, as well as the shields (Ancilia) which the Salii carried in their solemn processions. Furthermore, the annals were preserved here which the pontifex made up every year and in which the names of the highest magistrates were indicated, as well as the omens, the wars and the triumphs of the year, etc. The visible remains date largely from a restoration which the Consul Gnaeus Domitius Calvinus executed shortly after 36 B.C. This restoration consisted, for the most part, of solid blocks of marble; the west and south walls bore, both as a decoration and as an indication of the purpose of the structure, the list of the highest magistrates from Romulus to Caesar (the fasti consulares) as well as the triumphs of the same period. Many of these inscribed blocks of marble were found as late as the year 1546 in their original position, and are now stored in the Palazzo dei Conservatori.

These fragments as well as several pieces of entablature discovered through new excavations make it possible to effect a complete reconstruction of this part of the building (Fig. 19). The Regia before Calvinus was evidently larger though the remains of foundations of tufa blocks give us no satisfactory idea of it.

In front of the Regia stood the temple of Caesar and the arch of Augustus; the point where we began our description (see above, p. 14, f.).

FIG. 19. The Regia of Domitius Calvinus

We turn south, to the temple of Castor, of which three columns, never overturned, formed in the Middle Ages one of the proofs of the existence of the Forum.

This temple of the Dioscuri, Castor and Pollux, called Templum Castoris or Templum Castorum in Roman official language, had its origin in the early years of the Republic. It was vowed in the year 496 B.C. and dedicated in 484. The Roman legend related how in the battle of Lake Regillus in which the exiled Tarquins received their decisive blow, the

Dioscuri led the Roman troops to victory, and how they then themselves brought the good news to the City and watered their steeds at the sacred spring of Juturna. Therefore, this spot at the lower end of the market place was chosen as their shrine. The temple was repeatedly damaged and restored and the present remains (plate 22) date back in essentials to the restoration which Tiberius dedicated in 6 A.D. A lofty flight of steps led to the portico; three beautiful columns with capitals and entablatures are preserved which belonged to the left aisle. In the high substructures beneath the cella small chambers were found (in a good state of preservation, lying on the left side under the standing columns), which were perhaps used for practical purposes. It is known from inscriptions, for instance, that the Roman official bureau of weights and measures was in or near the temple of Castor.

East of this temple and separated from it by a street lies the sacred precinct of Juturna. In very ancient times a spring gushed forth at the foot of the Palatine and was caught in a basin (lacus); near-by stood a shrine with a statue of the nymph. The Lacus Juturnae (plate 23) is now an oblong basin in the centre of which a block of reticulated tufa rises, forming an island. At the time of excavation the basin was discovered to be filled up with fragments of marble and bits of sculpture which came in part from the surrounding buildings. Perhaps, therefore, the lovely marble altar which now stands on a step within the Lacus with reliefs on its four sides showing Zeus, Leda, the Dioscuri and a goddess of light (Selene-Helena?), belonged originally in the temple of Castor. A second marble altar now standing in front of the shrine (Aedicula) which bears on its architrave the inscription JUTURNAI S(acrum), of far interior workmanship, bears on its front a relief showing Juturna with her brother Turnus, known from Vergil as the leader of the Rutuli. In front of the Aedicula stands also a charming round well head (Puteal), by means of which the spring was likewise accessible. According to the inscription it was erected by the Curule Aedile Marcus Barbatius Pollio, presumably under Augustus. East of the Lacus, on the side towards the House of the Vestals is a room with walls of good brickwork and niches at the rear wall, which perhaps served for religious purposes. Numerous sculptural fragments found in the Lacus are preserved here; among those deserving attention are a reconstructed group of the Dioscuri with their steeds, in archaic style, perhaps executed in southern Italy in the fifth century B.C.; and also a statue of Aesculapius, the god of medicine. In later imperial times a part of this group of buildings served for practical uses, for according to the inscription on a marble pedestal standing here it contained among others the office of the municipal water supply (statio aquarum).

The rear of the shrine of Juturna touches the side wall of a chamber of good brick work, the front façade of which opens westward with a wide entrance portal. Its ancient purpose is uncertain, one might suppose it to be the shrine of Minerva which is frequently mentioned in connection with

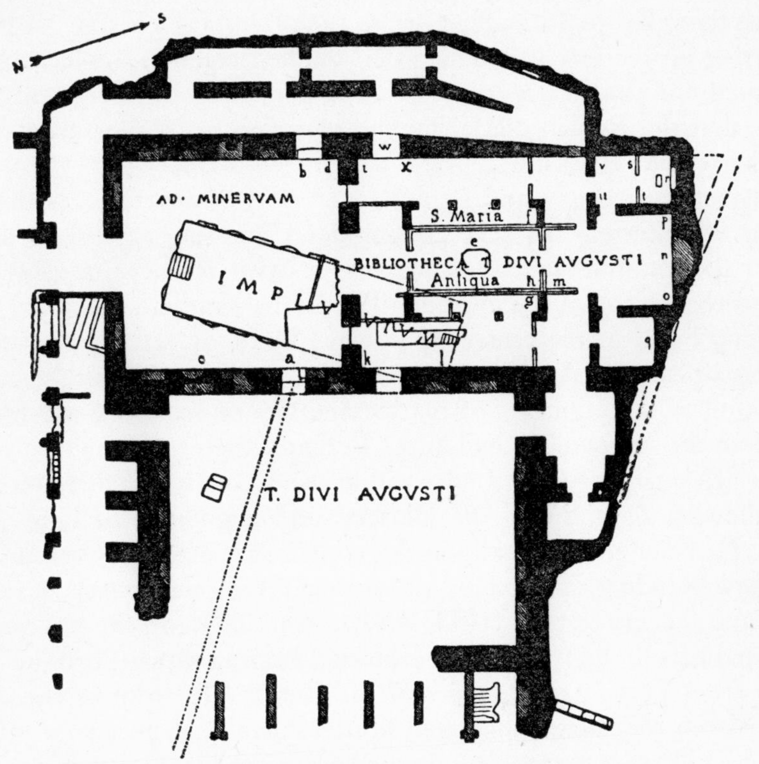

FIG. 20. Templum Divi Augusti and Library (S. Maria Antiqua)

the temple of Castor and that of Augustus. In Christian times, perhaps in the seventh century, it was transformed into an Oratory of the Forty Martyrs of Sebaste (in Armenia). Very badly damaged frescoes present the martyrdom of the forty Christian soldiers who met their death in Diocletian's persecution, and their glorification; and also tales of Anthony the Hermit.

To the right (south) of this room lies the entrance to a far larger building, a monument which was likewise transformed into a Christian church (Fig. 20 and plate 24). The ancient building consists of a forecourt and numerous halls and chambers grouped around a square atrium. It is connected with the large brick building, Templum Divi Augusti, by two small doors. It is extremely probable that this can be regarded as the library of Augustus' temple, which, together with the temple itself, was restored by Domitian after a fire. In the forecourt below the level of Domitian's structures were found remains of older buildings, notably a large water basin (impluvium) which may have belonged to a palace of Caligula. From the forecourt we enter the atrium which has three arched openings at either side supported on columns. From the left (east) room a wide gently sloping ramp rises in two turns to the Nova Via behind the House of the Vestals and continues on to the Clivus Victoriae and the imperial palaces. Behind the atrium we find a larger central chamber and two side rooms which may originally have been intended for storing the books.

The transformation of the building into a Christian church was accomplished at a very early date, at a period when there was still a great unwillingness to use pagan temples for the practice of the Christian religion notwithstanding a decided predilection for devoting ancient secular buildings to that use. The church built into the library bore the name of S. Maria Antiqua more than 1200 years ago, not because it was the oldest church in the city dedicated to the Virgin, for both S. Maria Maggiore and also S. Maria in Trastevere are considerably older, but still as one of the oldest and most venerated shrines to the Mother of God.

The numerous frescoes which make this church one of the most important repositories of ancient Christian art in Rome allow us also to draw positive conclusions in regard to the history of architecture; namely, that the church was in existence as early as the second half of the sixth century. The atrium with its two adjacent chambers was transformed into the central and side aisles; the larger chamber behind the atrium was utilized for presbytery and choir and the straight rear wall remained unchanged. It was not until later that it was breached for the construction of a semi-circular apse; and the smaller lateral chambers became chapels.

As early as the second half of the seventh century the frescoes were renewed; later Popes John VII (705–707), Zacharias (741–752), Paul I (757–765) and Hadrian I (772–795) acquired merit by the decoration of the church. In the eighth century S. Maria Antiqua was, it appears, given over to Greek monks, who at the time of the controversy over icons were forced to flee from Byzantium and found protection in Rome and a fertile field for their artistic activity. The presence of numerous Greek inscriptions on the frescoes is characteristic. Pictures which might be dated later than the middle of the ninth century are entirely wanting. Probably it was about this time that the decaying imperial palaces situated above the church began to present a constant danger.

It was for this reason that Pope Leo IV (845–853) established a new church to the Virgin a short distance away in the ruins of the temple of Venus and Rome and this was then called S. Maria Nova.

S. Maria Antiqua fell into ruins and was completely forgotten. The locality had a bad reputation, it was called *infernus* (accursed) and the legend of S. Sylvester tells about a subterranean lair where a fire-belching dragon dwelt which was rendered harmless by the saint; a mediaeval version of the Roman legend of the Lacus Curtius. Even before the 14th century we find a new church dedicated to the Virgin, called S. Maria de Inferno, which stood considerably above the level of the old one. But it is worthy of note that there never was a church to S. Silvestro in Lacu in spite of the legends about it told by scholars of the Renaissance. This new church which was later called S. Maria Libera Nos de Poenis Inferni or S. Maria Liberatrice was in existence until the year 1900.

Even the forecourt of the church is richly decorated with frescoes. In one picture Pope Hadrian I appears with the square blue nimbus which in the art of this period characterizes important living persons; according to which the pictures date from the period between 772 and 795. From the forecourt we enter the ancient atrium in the centre of which is preserved an octagonal brick base probably from a pulpit (ambo). Lying near it and belonging to it is an octagonal marble slab the edges of which bear the following inscription in both Latin and Greek: "John the servant of the Mother of God." The founder was Pope John VII (705–707), of whom his biographer relates that he decorated S. Maria Antiqua with paintings and erected a marble chancel in it. From the central aisle three steps lead up to the choir (schola cantorum) the screens of which are decorated with frescoes from the Old Testament (middle of the eighth century). Two pictures at the right are well preserved: the sick king Hezekiah with the Prophet Jeremiah and David as the conqueror of Goliath the giant. Beside the schola cantorum lies the presbytery, formerly the central hall of the library. On the rear wall three layers of frescoes, one above the other, can be distinguished (plate 25), the lowest of which dates back to a period when the rear wall had not yet been broken by the semi-circular apse. To the right of the apse, on the lowest layer, which is assigned to the sixth century, we see an enthroned Madonna adored by angels; this painting was later mutilated and lost the left half. On the second layer, assigned with probability to the second half of the seventh century, an Annunciation was pictured, and on the upper layer, which perhaps dates from the period of John VII, were presented church fathers with large golden halos. The apse itself was twice decorated, first under John VII and later under Paul I (757–765); the upper layer shows the Christ with angels and the Madonna. Above the apse in the lunette we have Christ on the Cross adored by angels in white garments and below a broad band with Greek inscriptions, the whole dating from the period of John VII.

To the left of the presbytery lies a chapel with particularly well preserved frescoes. In a niche above the altar we see a representation of the Crucifixion (plate 26), below the niche in the centre an enthroned Madonna (partly destroyed) with Peter and Paul, beside them the saints to whom the chapel was dedicated, the boy Quiricus and his mother Julitta. To the left of this group we have Pope Zacharias (741–752) wearing the square blue nimbus, to the right the Primicerius Theodotus, uncle of Pope Hadrian I (772–795) who also wears the square blue nimbus and holds a model of the church in his hands. On the side walls, above, we have the story of Quiricus and Julitta with legends in Latin. Among the remaining frescoes, all of which date back to the middle of the eighth century, a painting on the right wall below deserves attention, in which the Madonna is adored by a noble family, probably that of Theodotus the founder; likewise a second painting on the entrance wall, showing Theodotus holding two large wax torches in his hands as he kneels before Quiricus and Julitta.

Going from the chapel back into the left aisle in which the frescoes are well preserved, especially those in the lower half of the wall: in the centre we have Christ enthroned, His hand upraised in blessing, at His left nine Greek saints, at His right eleven Latin saints and church fathers, all with names and legends in Greek. Above is a cycle of paintings from the Old Testament beginning with the Creation and ending with the history of the patriarchs, but only a few of the later pictures, the history of Joseph (with Latin legends), are moderately well preserved. But in the right aisle and the adjoining chapel the frescoes are very few and those are badly damaged.

The entire group of buildings described above abuts on a far larger building, the mighty brick walls of which are preserved to a height of more than twenty metres (plate 27). The western façade facing on the Vicus Tuscus is almost entirely destroyed as well as the portico opposite which lies much lower. The principal room has niches for statues in the lower portion of the walls; it was probably covered by a wide-spanned wooden roof. We see in this building the cella of the Templum Divi Augusti in the form it received from a restoration under Domitian as may be recognized by numerous stamped bricks dated in his reign which were found in the walls. The original building, begun by Tiberius and dedicated by Caligula had more modest dimensions and, as it seems, a different orientation. This was destroyed in Nero's fire and magnificently restored by Domitian. Even at this time it was dedicated not only to the Founder of the Empire, but also to the deified emperors and empresses after him. A second restoration followed under Antoninus Pius (137–161), but nothing definite is known about its destruction. In Christian times this building was connected with the church, as is proved by remains of paintings on the east wall near the small doorways leading into the passageways, showing the figures of saints. It is a mistake to try, as was recently attempted, to account for this building as a forecourt of the imperial palaces, as it is not connected with them in any way. Besides, there is absolutely no other spot where the Templum Divi Augusti could be located: it is known to have stood below the west slope of the Palatine in the vicinity of the shrine to Minerva which was near the temple of Castor.

At the south side of the temple of Augustus, between the Vicus Tuscus and the Palatine remains of buildings came to light during the most recent excavations which served neither as living quarters nor for religious purposes. Single, disconnected vaulted chambers of tufa blocks not connected with one another are grouped about large courts. This is the type of large warehouses (horrea) such as were found in great numbers in every region of the Capital: they were used to store not only foodstuffs but for wares of all sorts, including furniture and other private property. In one of these courts, which in this instance are trapezoidal in shape to conform to the converging streets formed by the Vicus Tuscus in the valley and the Clivus Victoriae at the declivity of the Palatine, was found a marble pedestal which bears the name of the building, Horrea Germaniciana. This refers to its founding by Germanicus in the time of Augustus or Tiberius. The plan of these chambers was preserved on the city map of the time of Septimius Severus (Fig. 21), and according to the description of the city made in Constantine's time they were still standing in the middle of the fourth century.

The sacred precinct of the water deity Juturna borders on that of Vesta, the goddess of the hearth fire. The temple of Vesta and the dwelling house of the Vestals (Atrium Vestae) lie northeast of the precinct of Juturna, between the declivity of the Palatine and the Sacra Via.

The temple of Vesta, which, according to its founding is one of the

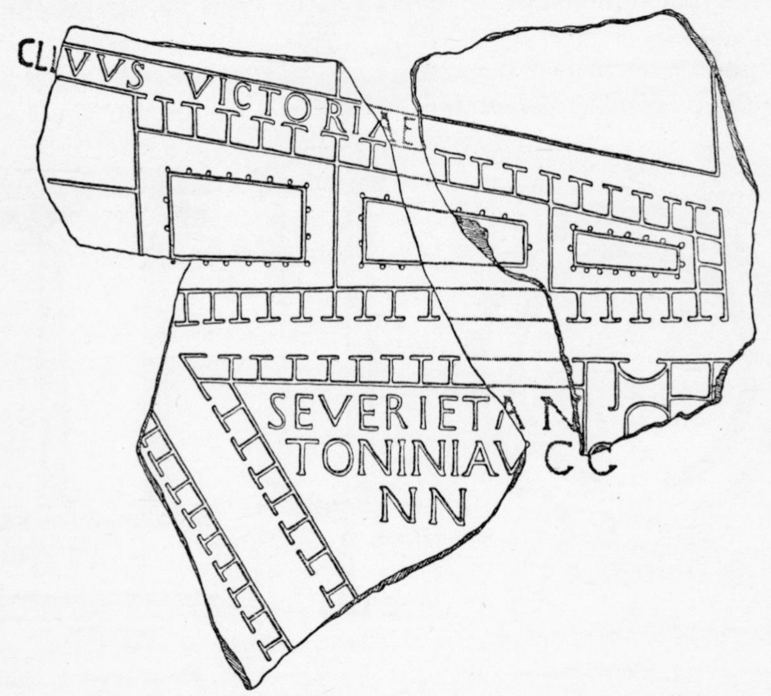

FIG. 21. Horrea Germaniciana on the Ancient Plan of the City

oldest temples in Rome, lies south of the Regia, separated from it by a street. It was a circular building and its shape was reminiscent of the oldest Italic peasant hut made of wattles and straw (see plate 41). Existing remains date from imperial times, principally from a restoration executed about 200 A.D. after a fire, by the wife of Septimius Severus, Julia Domna. The foundations, which are of concrete and tufa blocks, have a diameter of about fourteen metres (fifty Roman feet) (Fig. 22); upon them rose the cella, the diameter of which measures about nine metres (thirty Roman feet) surrounded by a colonnade of twenty Corinthian columns

(Fig. 23). The cella had a solid marble wall, probably without windows, as it received light from the door and through an opening in the summit of the roof. In the cella we find no cult statue but only a hearth in the centre, on which the Vestals were required to keep the sacred fire forever burning. The temple was strictly isolated, men (except the Pontifex Maximus) might never enter, and women only during the festival of Vesta in June. This isolation is clearly expressed also in the exterior of the building as can be seen in the representations on reliefs and on coins as well as from the remains.

Seventeen intercolumniations of the portico were closed by metal screens and the three opposite the entrance to the cella by wooden doors: traces

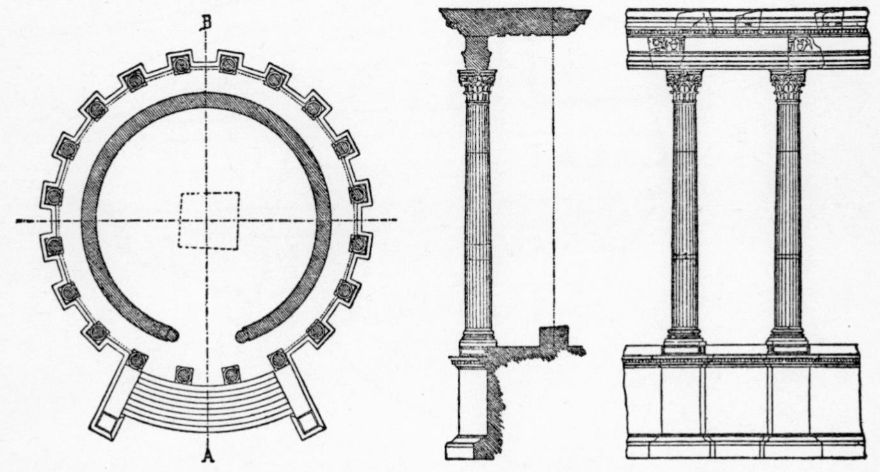

FIG. 22. Temple of Vesta, Ground plan

FIG. 23. Temple of Vesta, Portico

of the fastenings for the gratings and the door frames are still visible on some of the shafts of the columns. The colonnade, in addition to its decorative purpose, achieved great stability: the entablature, the coffered ceiling and the inner frieze of the cella formed one whole, consisting of large blocks, almost three metres in length, by means of which the cella wall and the bases of the columns were bound together in a uniform counterpoise for the wide-spanned roof. This tentlike roof, as we learn from representations on coins, had a sort of chimney set on it, probably of bronze, in the shape of a flower, which protected the interior and especially the hearth in the centre from rain (Fig. 24).

No statue of the goddess might stand in the temple itself, as ancient writers emphasize, but by way of compensation one was set up in a small shrine (aedicula) erected beside the temple (plate 28). The inscription on the architrave which, judging from the form of the letters, dates from the beginning of the second century A.D., attests the restoration of the shrine by the Senate and the People at the public expense. Beside the shrine a few steps lead to a little door, the entrance to the Atrium Vestae (plate 29).

FIG. 24. Temple of Vesta, Reconstruction

The dwelling of the six Vestal virgins is called Atrium Vestae from the principal room of the house, the large central courtyard. The cloistered seclusion in which the priestesses spent their lives within these walls is signalized by the entrance, which is an unpretentious side door instead of being a monumental portal in the main axis of the courtyard. In republican times the House of the Vestals had modest dimensions, beside the dwelling there was a sacred grove, lucus Vestae, which extended to the west corner of the Palatine and the lower end of the Nova Via. Of this earlier house of the Vestals only unconnected ruins underneath the level of the imperial buildings were identified; whatever is visible above the ground dates from the first to the third century A.D. The oldest part, dating from the first century, is the east end of the court containing the official rooms; the dwelling quarters and other domestic apartments on the south side and the west end belong to the middle of the second century, and those on the north side, towards the Sacra Via, probably date from a restoration of Septimius Severus after the great conflagration under Commodus (191 A.D.).

The centre of the court was embellished with gardens, perhaps to make up for the vanished grove: there are several large water basins in the long axis. The east end is largely taken up with a square vaulted chamber, the tablinum, so called, with three single cells at each side. It is supposed that one cell was assigned to each of the six priestesses where she could keep her sacred utensils, etc., while the central room served for the transaction of general official business. Beside the so-called tablinum lie two open courts, the one at the left is called the summer dining-room, the one at the right with a well and a sort of cellar built in served perhaps for household purposes. Domestic rooms are also to be found near this court in the south wing quite changed by late rebuilding: there is a well preserved mill and next to it what is probably a bakery. Other domestic rooms notably kitchens and store rooms lie in the west wing; the purpose of the badly damaged rooms in the north wing is still uncertain. The living quarters for the priestesses and their numerous servants lay in the upper stories: the house had at least three stories, maybe four (plate 30) on the side towards the Palatine, not counting the mezzanine over the ground floor.

The tablinum does not lie in the long axis of the court, and it is possible that the wings which were built or rebuilt at various times presented no symmetrical view. In order to cover up these irregularities effectively the court was surrounded by a colonnade, probably at the time of the reconstruction under Septimius Severus, consisting of two rows of columns, one above the other but without a floor between them. The columns in the lower set are of green-veined cipollino, those of the upper of red-veined breccia corallina. Numerous remains of columns and entablatures as well as the statues and honorary inscriptions for the head Vestals (Virgines Vestales Maximae) attest the magnificence of the equipment of the court. The inscriptions which can be dated begin with 201 A.D., the latest bear the dates 364 and 380 A.D. Constantine and his successors did not quite dare to abrogate the cult of Vesta and her priestesses, Gratian was the first to confiscate the estates of the Vestals in the year 382. It can be proved however that the house was inhabited again in later centuries, till the 10th century, at first, it would appear, by officials of the imperial court and later by those of the papal court.

The Sacra Via which runs along the north side of the House of the Vestals up to the Velia is lined on the right (south) side by brick buildings, shops and private houses. In imperial times it was one of the most elegant of the business streets of the Capital: in the inscriptions there is often mention especially of jewelers, goldsmiths, pearl dealers, sculptors, as well as florists, wreath makers and grocers *de Sacra Via.* The left side of the street is taken up with monuments of the later empire.

One of the monuments conspicuous for the excellent state of its preservation is the round temple which the Emperor Maxentius dedicated in the year 307 to Romulus his son (plate 31) who died in boyhood. It is a circular temple erected on a triangular piece of ground which was left over between the Sacra Via and the buildings of Vespasian's Forum Pacis which approached it. Accordingly, the temple was constructed as a rotunda with the back wall touching one of the adjoining buildings of the Forum Pacis. Furthermore, the irregularities of the site are skilfully hidden by an arched entrance porch flanked by two rectangular rooms with rounded apses. The entrance door is flanked by two porphyry columns which were taken from an older building, as was also the rich entablature above. The entablature has the same lovely decoration on the back, now hidden from view, as it has on the front. The bronze door is also ancient and its somewhat complicated arrangement for opening and closing is still in order.

The Heroon of Romulus is the first ancient temple in the Forum to have been used as a Christian church. Pope Felix IV (527–530) made it into the portico of a church which he dedicated to the martyrs Cosmas and Damianus in the adjoining wing of the Forum Pacis mentioned above. The east wall of this room, running lengthwise towards the basilica of Constantine is of excellent masonry of Vespasian's day and is especially well preserved. In modern times it was quite gratuitously called Templum Sacrae Urbis because the marble plan of the City (Forma Urbis Romae) was cut into the marble facing of the wall on the north side, i.e. the one toward the temple of Peace, as a decoration in the time of Septimius Severus (193–211 A.D.). This is probably the part once mentioned as the library of the temple of Peace. In the interior of the chamber until well into the 16th century, a great part of the ancient marble facing was still on the walls, with mosaic work in rich patterns with figures and other designs.

When the chamber was transformed into a church it was diminished a third in size by the construction of a wall with an apse and between the chamber itself and the rotunda, now changed into a portico, a door was broken through the south wall. The mosaics in the apse, dating from the time of the founder, are among the best early Christian work of this kind in Rome. The church existed in this form until the time of Urban VIII (1623–1644), who had it raised a whole story to correspond to the modern street level because of the danger of damage from dampness due to its lying so low. The square main room is still at this level, but the rotunda was restored to the ancient level of the Sacra Via by the recent excavations.

On the north side of the Sacra Via beside the Templum Divi Romuli traces of buildings erected by Nero have lately been identified, for he had included this whole region in his Golden House. The Sacra Via, as regulated by Nero, led to one of the main entrances of this gigantic pile, and in a forecourt on the summit of the Velia he had erected the colossal bronze statue of himself as the sun god. This group of buildings disappeared under his successors: Domitian (81–96) established large storehouses for oriental wares, especially spices (horrea piperataria), on the north side of the street. They existed until the close of the third century, at the beginning of the fourth century Maxentius began a new basilica at this spot which surpassed all others in size (plate 32), and Constantine completed it. This building is entirely different in construction from the older basilicas with their columns and pillars and is rather a development of the large central halls of the imperial Thermae, of which the central hall of the baths of Diocletian, now the church of S. Maria degli Angeli, furnishes the best example in Rome. This basilica (Fig. 25) has three aisles, the original main entrance with a portico is at the east, towards the Colosseum, and the apse is at the opposite (west) wall. This structure, built by Maxentius, was altered, perhaps by Constantine, in such a way that a second entrance was made at the south (Sacra Via) and opposite it a second apse was built into the aisle on the north side. Within, only four mighty pillars support the arches of the gigantic hall, the area of which is about three times that of the Basilica Julia with its seventy-four interior supports. In front of the pillars there were colossal columns of white marble with Corinthian capitals; the last of them, which still frequently appears in drawings and etchings of the 16th century (plate 33), was transferred by

Pope Paul V in 1611 to the Piazza in front of S. Maria Maggiore where it now supports a statue of the Madonna. In the original apse at the west

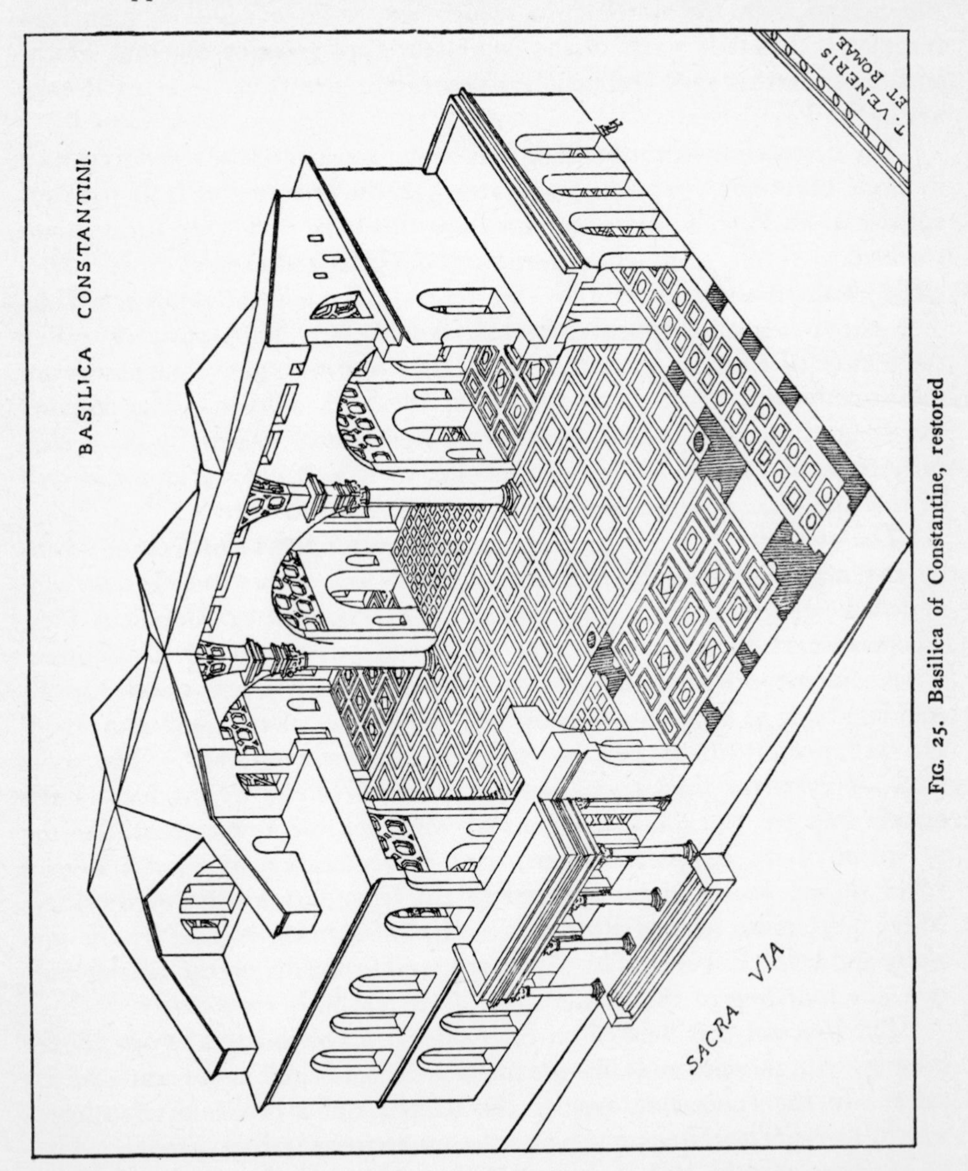

FIG. 25. Basilica of Constantine, restored

end there was formerly a colossal seated statue of Constantine, the head, arms and legs of which were found here about 1490 and are now preserved in the courtyard of the Palazzo dei Conservatori on the Capitol. In front of the apse beneath the level of the basilica remains of older brickwork covered with colored stucco are visible, belonging perhaps to the Horrea Piperataria. In the north apse, which was a later addition, numerous fragments especially parts of the entablature are grouped together which, with their extravagant and tasteless decoration attest the decay of Roman art in the late period.

The destruction of the building was begun as early as the seventh century by Pope Honorius (625–638) who removed the bronze tiles from the roof for use in St. Peter's. The structure was too huge to be transformed into a church or taken for practical purposes. Neglect and natural events, especially earthquakes, early laid low the central nave and the south side aisle. The north side aisle which remained standing was inappropriately called the temple of Peace in the late Middle Ages and the correct name was not substituted for it until the beginning of the 19th century. The remains were eagerly studied by architects of the Renaissance, especially the beautifully coffered vaulted ceiling. Bramante, as is well known, used the arch of the side aisle as a model for the main nave of St. Peter's.

The summit of the Velia was occupied, after the second century A.D. by the magnificent double temple of Venus and Rome, which was built and dedicated in 135 A.D. by Hadrian and completed by Antoninus Pius. The sanctuary had two cellas, the one on the west, towards the Forum, was dedicated to Roma, on the east, to Venus. The two semi-circular apses, standing back to back, in which the colossal statues of the goddesses stood, are well preserved, as well as parts of the adjoining walls. The walls were of excellent brickwork, faced with solid blocks of marble. Each temple had ten Corinthian columns of white marble at the front. In the pediment of the temple of Roma, as a representation of it on a Roman relief shows, were reliefs representing the legendary history of the City: Mars descending toward Rhea Silvia, the twins being suckled by the she-wolf, and being discovered by shepherds, and probably, on the missing portion, the founding of the City.

The precinct was flanked on each side by a colonnade of gray granite columns with porches built like pavilions at the ends and in the centre of the sides. In the transverse axis of the temple stood two colossal columns which, as representations on coins show, supported statues, probably those of Hadrian and his wife Sabina; the foundations and a fragment of the cipollino column from the north axis are preserved.

While the temple on the west side lies only a few steps above the Sacra

Via, the terrace on the opposite side rises to a considerable height (plate 34). In front of it, to the right (north) a pedestal for a gigantic statue is preserved; on it, after Hadrian's day, stood the colossal sun god of Nero, which was transferred from its original site by order of the emperor. The plan to erect a similar gigantic statue of Luna on the other corner was never carried out. The colossus survived the fall of paganism; a writer of the seventh century (the Venerable Bede) has left us the saying of the pilgrims: "While the colossus stands, Rome shall stand; when the colossus falls, Rome shall fall and with Rome, the world," though this is usually erroneously quoted as referring to the Colosseum.

Beside the temple of Roma, as the street turns to the right and leads to the so-called Palatine Plaza (Area Palatina) and the imperial palaces, rises the triumphal arch of Titus (plate 35). It celebrates the deeds of the emperor in the war with the Jews (69–70) but it was not dedicated until after his death and more than a decade later (81). This is proved not only by the inscription, which speaks of the emperor as Divus, but also by the relief in the centre of the vaulting which shows the Genius of the emperor borne to heaven by an eagle. The reliefs on the inner side of the passage represent the triumphal procession: to the left, the emperor in the triumphal car; to the right, the trophies from the temple at Jerusalem. It was the latter relief which gave the arch its name in the Middle Ages: the Arch of the Seven Branched Candlestick (Arcus Septem Lucernarum). At that time the arch was built into the fortifications which closed the passage between S. Maria Nova and the Palatine. The street ran deeper than the ancient Sacra Via, as can be seen from the foundations, and thus it was possible to build a chamber in the upper half of the passage by tapering in a ceiling or a shallow arch.

In the course of these additions the lower half of the beautiful reliefs depicting the triumph was damaged. A part of the insertions and of the additions was removed by the end of the 15th century, though the arch was not entirely freed from encumbrances till 1822. In the course of this work, the pillars at the sides were discovered to be so badly damaged that it was necessary to reconstruct them entirely and this work was very skilfully executed under the direction of Valadier. Only the central marble portion of the arch is ancient, and can easily be distinguished from the repairs and reconstructions carried out in travertine. The temple of Jupiter Stator which stood beside the arch belongs to the Palatine, according to the ancient division of the City (see below, p. 66).

BURIAL AND EXCAVATION OF THE FORUM

EVEN though the removal of the imperial residence from Rome to Byzantium by Constantine in 330 signifies the beginning of the destruction of the old capital, still throughout the fourth and fifth centuries the emperor and the authorities endeavored to protect the monuments of the venerable Forum from destruction. The temples were of course closed under Emperor Constantius (346), but they were preserved as historic monuments or for practical purposes (cf. the remarks on the temples of Caesar and Saturn, p. 15 f. and p. 20). In the fifth century the Forum suffered through hostile invasions (the Goths under Alaric 410, the Vandals under Genseric, 455) and through natural events (earthquake, 442); but even after the fall of the western Roman Empire (476) the Ostrogothic kings, especially the vigorous Theodoric (483–526) tried to keep the buildings of the capital in repair, as far as the means and the artistic ability of those times permitted.

It was at this epoch that the Christian religion began to gain a foothold in the Forum. The first building which was dedicated to it (between 526 and 530) is the Heroon of Romulus, the son of an emperor, on the Sacra Via; and it was probably not much later that the church of S. Maria Antiqua was established in the library of the temple of Augustus. Then in the seventh century ancient buildings were more and more frequently used as Christian churches: in the Senate House the churches of S. Adriano (625–638) and S. Martina found an abiding place; an Oratory of Saints Sergius and Bacchus crept into the portico of the temple of Concord; and a similar shrine to the Apostles Peter and Paul into the portico of the temple of Venus and Rome. Traffic was maintained in the Forum in the eighth century and the beginning of the following century approximately at the ancient level, as is attested by the curious description of the City for which we are indebted to a German pilgrim of the time of Charlemagne, as well as by the condition of the monuments (private buildings in the Basilica Aemilia and the church in the west aisle of the Basilica Julia).

In the 10th and 11th centuries the destruction and burial of the Forum seem to have progressed enormously though the meagre chronicles of that time do not permit us to learn the details. However, about the middle of the 12th century we find the Forum a pathless waste.

The solemn papal processions, concerning which contemporary documents give exact details avoided the Forum and made a wide detour through the fora of Augustus and Nerva in order to go from the arch of Severus to the arch of Titus. The gradual rise of the ground can be observed especially well in the case of the façade of the church of S. Adriano which it was necessary to set about three metres higher in the 11th or beginning of the 12th century (cf. above, p. 30). On many of the ancient monuments, the triumphal arches, for instance, the Roman barons of that day built their fortified towers and battlements and they naturally took the material for their buildings largely from ruins in the vicinity. During the constant feuds these buildings were not seldom destroyed and their débris elevated the ground still further.

In the 14th century, at the time when the church government was removed to France, Rome was torn by party strife and stricken by pestilence and suffered the annihilation of her population and the destruction of her culture. But towards the end of the century better times began for the city with the return of the popes from Avignon and the healing of the schism in the church.

A new period of great activity began in the construction of churches and of private buildings, with one bad result, indeed, that many ruins of the old city served as quarries, among them the Forum. And this plundering had not ceased when, in the 15th and 16th centuries the study of ancient architecture and of Roman history began to flourish. Many of the mediaeval buildings also disappeared: The construction of a triumphal way in honor of the victorious return of the Emperor Charles V from Tunis by Pope Paul III in 1536 produced a lasting effect as the road ran from the arch of Titus to the arch of Severus and this necessitated the tearing down of numerous buildings which were in the way. After that the Forum was once again included in the city traffic though even now the herds of cattle from the Campagna settled down on this historic spot and the common name for it was Campo Vaccino, while the name of Forum Romanum was so far forgotten that for centuries it was erroneously believed to be in an entirely different locality.

A particularly good idea of the condition of the Forum at the time of the entrance into Rome of Charles V is presented in the drawings of a Flemish artist, Martin van Heemskerck, who spent some time in Rome between 1534 and 1536. One of these views, which is reproduced in the folding plate, (36 a), the artist took from the foot of the Capitoline, standing on the pile of débris in front of the Tabularium. The columns of the temple of Vespasian are buried to half their height in this pile; and in front of the temple, towards the arch of Severus, can be seen the church of SS. Sergio e Bacco with the façade toward the Forum and the apse toward the Capitoline. The rubbish rises high enough to cover the bases of the pillars of the arch of Severus and on the left corner of the attic there rests an embattled tower. The column of Phocas is buried in débris up to the base of the shaft and beside it are mean houses. Beyond it in the distance we can see the arch of Titus built into high walls, to the right the Torre Cartularia, to the left the bell tower of S. Maria Nova, and beside it the top story of the Colosseum.

In the 16th century there was as yet no thought of scientific investigation of the Forum by means of excavation. Whenever picks and spades were used it was for the acquisition of marble and travertine for new buildings, or what was worse, for the lime kiln. Occasionally a few beautiful architectural fragments or noteworthy inscriptions were rescued—the soil of the Forum has never produced a rich crop of statues or reliefs—but the greater part of it was dedicated to destruction. It was especially under Pope Paul III (1534–1550) that the monuments in the Forum suffered considerable damage through similar plundering of the buildings; and as contemporary documents and accounts show, the searchers after building materials carried on their work of destruction on almost every spot from the slope of the Capitoline to the arch of Titus.

In the 17th century the Forum no longer offered booty as a reward for digging, and so the depredations of buildings ceased, but so also did the occasional finds. The magnificent avenue of elm trees stretching in a perfectly straight line from the arch of Severus to the arch of Titus was characteristic of the appearance of the area of the Forum after about 1650. In the area of the Forum itself there were merely a few hovels and the herds of cattle camped on it; and in 1565 an artistic fountain was erected for watering the cattle beside the three columns of the temple of

Castor. This aspect of the Forum had scarcely changed in the 18th century, as is shown in the reproduction of the Piranesi etching in plate 36. The investigators of that time had no idea that one of the most important of the monuments of ancient Rome lay concealed beneath the Campo Vaccino; indeed, they believed that the Forum was situated under the hospital della Consolazione or farther west, while they thought that the Sacra Via, running between the arches of Severus and Titus was entirely separated from the Forum. These two triumphal arches, as well as the temple of Faustina, were the only monuments which could not be robbed of their correct names, thanks to their inscriptions. On the other hand, the temple of Saturn was mostly called the temple of Concord, and the temple of Vespasian temple of Jupiter Tonans; the temple of Castor was thought to be that of Jupiter Stator, and the column of Phocas was called Columna Maenia.

A change took place after the end of the 18th century. The complete revival of the study of archaeology was effected by the activity of J. J. Winckelmann who taught us the value of methodical excavation. To Carlo Fea, the third successor to Winckelmann as papal Commissario delle Antichità belongs the credit for planning and for actually beginning a systematic uncovering of the Forum. Hampered as he was by conditions in his day, he was naturally forced to limit himself to excavating a few conspicuous monuments, and the appearance of the Forum towards the end of his period of activity is represented by a lovely engraving by E. Fries (1824, reproduced on plate 37). We see that the arch of Severus has been laid bare down to the ancient level, the houses near the column of Phocas have disappeared, thus disclosing the base of the column with its inscription; and at the temple of Castor also the ancient level has been reached. Similar excavation was carried on in the Basilica Julia and near the temple of Concord, though these are not visible in the picture. But these excavations were all isolated trenches, deep holes with or without balustrades and the greater part of the Campo Vaccino with its avenue of elm trees remained undisturbed.

Considerable progress was made under Leo XII when Antonio Nibby took over the direction of the excavation of the Forum from 1827–1834. It was at this time that the entire slope of the Capitoline and the substructures of the Tabularium were laid bare, and the excavations at the arch of Severus, at the column of Phocas and in the Basilica Julia were extended and were all connected. In the following decades the clearing of the greater part of the Basilica Julia in 1848–49 is worthy of special mention. But even in 1860 the Forum still bore, as plate 38 shows, its old name of Campo Vaccino, and justly so. For only the west half of the ancient Forum was uncovered and it was separated from the temples below the Tabularium by a highway running up to the Piazza del Campidoglio.

Conditions changed after 1870 when the government of the new Kingdom of Italy took charge of the excavations. Pietro Rosa who had acquired great merit for his uncovering of the palaces of the Caesars on the Palatine, was entrusted with the direction of the work, and between 1871 and 1876 he entirely excavated the Basilica Julia and also the central part of the Forum as far as the temples of Castor and Faustina. Under G. Fiorelli, Rosa's successor, the work was extended along the Sacra Via from the temple of Faustina to the arch of Titus (1878–1880) though the entire group of remains was cut into three parts by two roads, one of which led from the arch of Severus to the Capitoline, the other from S. Lorenzo in Miranda to S. Maria Liberatrice. Plate 39 presents the Forum in this condition.

In the year 1882 the Minister, Baccelli, had these two streets removed, so that for the first and only time all the ruins of the Forum and the Sacra Via were united in one imposing whole. Considerations of traffic in modern times made it impossible to preserve the Forum in this condition. The excavations were continued, especially in the eastern part, where, under the direction of R. Lanciani the House of the Vestals was uncovered in 1884–85. Then another period of inactivity set in lasting thirteen years, during which only a few monuments were investigated with care. These were the Rostra, Regia, temple of Castor and arch of Augustus. The extent of the territory cleared at that time is shown in plate 40, which was made from a photograph taken from a balloon in 1898.

At the end of 1898 Giacomo Boni took over the direction of the excavations and pursued them for the next six years with no less energy than success. He doubled the area previously uncovered by the excavation of the Basilica Aemilia on the north side, the precinct of Juturna, the temple of Augustus and the library (as well as the church of S. Maria Antiqua), and the buildings on the Sacra Via as far as the arch of Titus. One point of particular importance is that Boni's investigations were not limited like most of the earlier ones, to the upper ancient level of the Empire, but methodically kept on down to the lowest levels. As a consequence, unknown monuments of great value were discovered, though the ground had been worked so many times. Among these monuments were the so-called grave of Romulus with the archaic cippus, the old necropolis, the Lacus Curtius, the pedestal of Domitian, etc. Since 1904 another pause has ensued, though there are many problems connected with the topography of the Forum which can be solved only by an investigation of the ground, and it is to be hoped that the solution will some day be found upon resuming operations.

THE PALATINE BEFORE IMPERIAL TIMES

According to the unanimous tradition of antiquity the Palatine Hill was the primitive centre of the City of Rome, and indeed it presents more favorable conditions for the laying out of an archaic city than any other of the seven hills. On three sides—east, south and west—it declines sharply, about thirty metres, into the neighboring valleys, and towards the north it was connected with the summit of the Esquiline by a narrow ridge, the Velia, which has gradually been levelled down. Two of the surrounding valleys, the Velabrum to the west and the valley of the Circus to the south, were originally traversed by brooks. Their winding course, frequently stagnant, turned the basins of the valleys into swamps by means of which the position of the heights was much strengthened. The summit itself had two peaks, Palatium to the east and Cermalus to the west, and presented an adequate space for an archaic settlement, not too large. The settlement lay near enough to the river to dominate the crossing while the narrow plain below was well adapted as the place for trading with the neighboring settlers at the oldest market, the Forum Boarium.

On the Palatine Hill Roman legend localized numerous reminders of the founders of the City and of its founding. It was in the swampy valley of the Velabrum when it was flooded, according to the legend, that the little chest containing the twins Romulus and Remus, who had been exposed, drifted to land at the fostering fig tree (Ficus Ruminalis); and it was in the wolf's den (Lupercal) at the foot of the hill that the twins were nourished by the she-wolf and later rescued by the shepherd Faustulus. On the summit of the hill the hut of Faustulus was shown, in which Romulus himself was supposed to have lived later. All of these spots, religiously maintained and variously adorned were still in existence as late as Constantine's day, that is, into Christian times. Today no remains are to be seen. The hut of Romulus, according to ancient witnesses, must have stood near the west corner of the Palatine in the vicinity of the Magna Mater temple though none of the stone foundations discovered at this spot can be connected with it with any certainty; and the declivity of the hill between

S. Teodoro and S. Anastasia where the Ficus Ruminalis and the Lupercal are to be sought is still covered with rubbish as high as a house. The so-called Capanna di Romolo (hut of Romulus) which now stands (plate 41) behind the Villa Mills, a considerable distance away from the Magna Mater temple, is a modern reconstruction erected especially on the analogy of the hut-shaped ash urns from Latin graves.

After Romulus had founded his city (Roma Quadrata), so the legend continues, and had named it after himself, he built a wall around it. This wall had two gates, Porta Mugonia, also called Porta Vetus Palatii, in the centre of the north side, opening on the Velia; and Porta Romana, probably signifying Water Gate from the old name of the Tiber, Rumon, leading to the valley of the Circus. The location of both can be approximately established. The former lay on the so-called Area Palatina not far from the arch of Titus, the latter, near the southwest corner not far from the church of S. Anastasia. Many remains of a wall of large brown tufa blocks, especially on the west side over the Velabrum, were formerly supposed to belong to the oldest fortification of the Palatine, but recent investigation regards them more correctly as buttresses from republican or perhaps even from early imperial times. A few courses of small flat tufa blocks near the west corner over the valley of the Circus are the best preserved and visible remains of the old fortification of the hill. A flight of steps on the south side running up from the valley of the Circus was called Scalae Caci after the legendary giant who was supposed to have hidden in his den at the declivity of the hill the cattle of Geryon which he stole from Hercules, and to have suffered punishment at the hands of the hero. Remains of these so-called steps of Cacus are preserved; at the top they are barred by a gateway the foundations of which are still visible (plate 42). At the summit of the hill close by numerous remains of foundations of large tufa blocks and also remains of archaic graves have been identified. Worthy of note among the remains is a very old circular cistern, of flat tufa blocks constructed at a time when the art of vaulting was still unknown: the upper part is formed by projecting courses of stone (in a corbelled vault). This unpretentious monument is among the oldest preserved not alone on the Palatine but in all Rome. Later the cistern fell into disuse and the lower half of it was filled up by a foundation of large tufa blocks which continues on outside of the cistern towards the so-called steps of Cacus. And here it becomes obvious that structures of large blocks which students formerly liked to call "Romulean" are really to be dated as from a much later period, perhaps not earlier than the fourth century B.C.

Now even though there are very scanty traces of a special fortification of the Palatine Hill, still we cannot doubt that one existed. Of course it is possible that even at the time of the invasion of the Gauls (390 B.C.) the fortification may have been neglected and have been worthless for the defence of the City; it was entirely abandoned after the City had been completely fortified in the middle of the fourth century by the so-called Servian Wall.

The Gallic invasion was commemorated by a monument at the foot of the Palatine in the shape of an altar dedicated to that mysterious deity Aius Locutius, who had called out to the Romans in the night to warn them of the danger that threatened. It is often assumed that an ancient altar now standing under the west corner (plate 43) which, according to the inscription, was rebuilt by a praetor C. Sextius Calvinus (about 100 B.C.) had some connection with this deity. It is true that the spot where this miracle is supposed to have taken place—the lower end of the Nova Via above the precinct of Vesta—is rather far from the present position of the altar and furthermore it does not bear the name of Aius Locutius but is dedicated to "the deity whether male or female." In any case it is a particularly well-preserved example of an archaic Roman sacrificial altar.

The monuments of antiquity on the Palatine which are mentioned by ancient authors are almost exclusively sanctuaries: the temple of Victoria, supposed to have been founded by Evander the Arcadian, who was said to have settled on the Palatine even before Romulus; the temple of Jupiter Victor erected by the Consul Fabius Maximus Rullianus after the battle at Sentinum in 295 B.C. which decided Rome's supremacy in Italy; and finally, the temple of Magna Mater, vowed towards the end of the Second Punic War (204 B.C.) and built after the victorious close of the war (dedicated 191 B.C.). The temple of Victoria should be found at the west slope, on the street leading up to the summit which was named for the temple, somewhat above the church of S. Teodoro; the remains of a substructure with a broad stairway lying near the southern edge with its façade overlooking the valley of the Circus (plate 44) are ascribed with some probability to the temple of Jupiter Victor. Recent attempts to ascribe them to the Augustan temple of Apollo contradict the clear testimony of ancient authors.

More important remains are preserved of the temple of Magna Mater, the great Phrygian mother of the gods. It is interesting as an example of a Roman temple built in republican times entirely of native materials without the use of marble and maintained throughout the entire Empire in this archaic form. It stands near the south corner of the Palatine above the so-called steps of Cacus (plate 45, above), picturesquely covered over by a grove of evergreen oak. The lofty concrete substructure is well preserved; an unusually high and broad flight of steps led up to the pronaos (Fig. 26). The temple had six Corinthian columns of peperino in front, numerous fragments of the shafts and capitals have been found, still showing remains

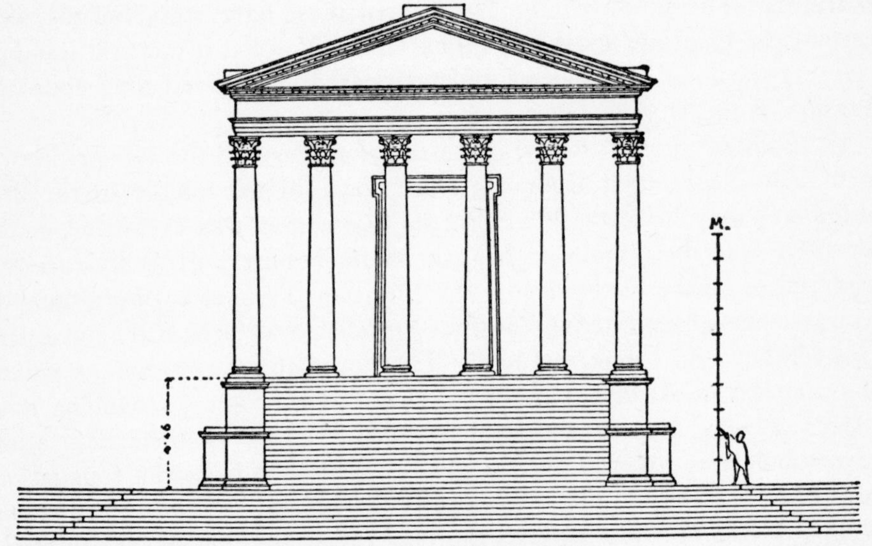

FIG. 26. Temple of Magna Mater

of the stucco facing in which all the finer forms were modelled. The cella contained no statue of the goddess, but only the black stone, probably a meteorite, which the Romans had received from Pessinus in Phrygia. However, representations of the Magna Mater were not wanting in the neighborhood; indeed there is one statue well preserved except for the head, a seated figure, larger than life size which was found at the upper end of the so-called steps of Cacus and now stands at the right side of the temple.

With this foreign cult unfamiliar usages from the Orient were also introduced into Rome: the festivals of the Magna Mater called by the Greek name of Megalesia were distinguished by many peculiarities foreign to the religion of Italy. Among others, they were solemnized with scenic plays, the theatre for which lay on the Palatine, in front of the temple. Plautus and Terence presented many of their pieces for the first time at these festivals and the large flight of steps at the front of the temple was very well suited for the spectators.

The hill on which the City first developed remained for centuries, to the end of the republican era, a well-inhabited, fashionable quarter. Many names from Rome's aristocracy appear among the householders on the Palatine: we have the orator Crassus; Lutatius Catulus, the conqueror of the Cimbri; Clodius the Tribune of the People and Marcus Tullius Cicero the orator. The house of the last named must have stood on the west corner of the Palatine, above the House of the Vestals; it was still standing as late as the time of Tiberius and was perhaps removed only upon the expansion of the Domus Tiberiana.

An excellent idea of the arrangement of rooms and the artistic decoration of a well-appointed Roman private house of the middle of the first century B.C. may be gathered from the house that was excavated in the year 1869 near the temple of Magna Mater, which is probably correctly considered to be the birthplace of the Emperor Tiberius. Inscriptions on lead water pipes found here prove that the house was later in the possession of his mother, the Empress Livia. The house faced east, where we can still recognize an atrium of the usual shape with rooms surrounding it on all sides, which have, of course, been plundered of all their decoration. The vestibule was covered over in the first century A.D. by the foundations of the Flavian palace. There are, however, several well-preserved rooms adjoining a second court towards the rear which are now incorrectly designated as Tablinum and as Ala dextra and sinistra. They are approached through a passage leading down, the original back door of the house. The rooms are decorated in the style which is commonly designated in Pompeii as the second or architectural style which was the reigning style in that city about the middle of the first century B.C. The wall paintings represent structures which one might imagine as really built of solid materials, not merely imaginary buildings like those of the fourth style with spindling columns and airy little temples; the frescoes imitate a facing of colored marble, serpentine and porphyry. This style employs two methods of introducing figure compositions: either the wall is apparently broken through by large windows or by irregular openings which allow a view into the open air and so make the room appear larger; or else small figures are set on the painted socles.

In the middle room on the court, the so-called tablinum (plate 46), both methods have been employed. On the right wall a large, painted window with a pediment above it gives a view of a landscape in which Io, transformed into a cow—the transformation is indicated only by two little horns above the forehead—is being watched by Argos of the hundred eyes, while Mercury hastens to her rescue. On the same wall a second false opening looks out on a street with charmingly unsymmetrical houses, balconies and porches. In the centre of the rear wall one saw, likewise through a false window, a seascape with Acis, Galatea and Polyphemus as figures, but this picture is badly damaged. On the moulding on the right wall there are apparently several pictures representing sacrificial scenes and ladies at their toilet, and according to ancient usage they are protected by shutters, like mediaeval altar pictures.

In the two side rooms there are no figures in the pictures but the fresco in the left chamber imitates in the lower half a facing of marble, porphyry and serpentine, in the upper part false windows permit a view of a surrounding portico, in the window openings we see fantastic pictures, so-called grotesques, made by combining the tendrils of vines with human figures. The chamber at the right (plate 47) has a background simulating a marble wall with charming festoons of foliage and fruit vines on which musical instruments are suspended, and above this a delicate frieze with landscapes, yellow on yellow. Another room on the south side of the court is usually called the dining-room (triclinium), because of the objects represented in the wall paintings; in the centre of the best preserved side wall there is a view of a shrine to Diana with trophies of the chase, boars' heads, deer's horns, etc., while on the moulding of the other side wall are painted large glass dishes with fruit. These rooms were still in the possession of the emperor in the time of Domitian, as the inscriptions on the water-supply pipes show, and perhaps they were purposely preserved in their original condition to commemorate the first empress and her son.

The birthplace of Augustus also stood on the Palatine and he likewise lived here as a private individual. "He inhabited the house," says his biographer (Suetonius), "which had formerly belonged to Hortensius the orator; it was distinguished neither for size nor for elegance, it had but few rooms with peperino columns, and it had no marble decoration nor artistic mosaic floors in any chamber."

Later when Octavianus became one of the rulers of the state after his victory over Sextus Pompeius (36 B.C.), he enlarged and improved this house. The building was struck by lightning, which soothsayers interpreted as denoting that the god Apollo had selected this spot as a residence for himself. As a consequence the emperor enlarged the plot by purchasing the adjoining houses and began the construction of a magnificent temple which with its annexes took up the entire east corner of the hill. Two years after the victory at Actium, which the emperor ascribed to the favor of his tutelary divinity, the temple was dedicated (Oct. 9, 28 B.C.). This was a building such as Rome had never yet beheld, made of solid blocks of marble which the recently opened quarries at Carrara furnished. But it was really this magnificence that spelled its doom. The temple outlived the fall of paganism, to be sure, and indeed it was again opened for religious observance under Julian the Apostate; but on the same night in which Julian met his death in distant Syria (March 18, 363 A.D.) a fire broke out in the temple of Apollo which found ample food for its flames in the enormous wooden roof. The flames reduced the blocks of marble to lime and the whole building, including its rich art treasures was completely destroyed, and not a trace of it remained. On the spot where it stood, which is occupied today by the little church of S. Maria (or S. Sebastiano) in Pallara, there are neither remains to be seen nor were any found in previous centuries. Only the brick substructures of the space around the temple, Area Apollinis, have been preserved, and with them a fragment of the entrance to the Area Palatina. Ancient writers praise the magnificence of this area around the temple which was surrounded by a portico of columns of a golden yellow Numidian marble (giallo antico) and richly adorned with works of art. From the colonnades one entered the two library buildings for Greek and for Latin literature which Augustus established in connection with the temple and which have likewise completely disappeared.

After Augustus had dedicated the site of his first home to Apollo, he began to build a new house, much larger and more magnificent, in the centre of the hill, and not much later Tiberius, his adopted son and successor to the throne, established a second palace on the west side above the valley of the Velabrum. These two palaces were enlarged and joined by means of additional buildings, by succeeding emperors, until they gradually took up the entire surface of the hill. As late as the fourth century the name Domus Augustiana et Tiberiana denoted the entire group of imperial palaces the ruins of which today give the Palatine its physiognomy.

THE IMPERIAL PALACES ON THE PALATINE

THE road from the Forum to the imperial palaces is graphically described by a contemporary of Augustus, the poet Ovid, in the first poem of the third book of his Elegies (Tristia) which he sends to the Capital from his place of exile on the Black Sea. A kind citizen leads the stranger up the Sacred Way past the Regia and the temple of Vesta. Then he turns to the right and points out the gate of the Palatine, the temple of Stator and a shrine which recalls the founding of Rome. The visitor stands there in admiration and sees, from the same spot, the façade of the imperial dwelling, decked with laurel and oak, the temple of Apollo and the library in which there is no room for the work of the poet who has fallen into disgrace.

Nor is it difficult today to follow the poet's route, since most of the monuments mentioned by him can still be identified with reasonable certainty. Today, however, the summit of the Velia is more strikingly characterized by the arch of Titus than by the temple of Stator, and the little shrine on the Area Palatina in which Romulus deposited the sacred utensils used in the founding of the City is still buried deep in the débris; but the temple of Stator, the emperor's palace and the sanctuary of Apollo, though in ruins and partly in altered form, are still before our eyes.

The temple of Stator was, according to the legend, vowed by Romulus when the Romans were hard pressed by the Sabines not far from the Porta Mugonia in the battle that followed the rape of their women. The foundations of the sanctuary were preserved because in the Middle Ages a fortified tower (Torre Cartularia) was erected upon it which served for a time to preserve the papal archives. A representation on a Roman relief shows that the temple had six columns on the front and was in the Corinthian style.

The spot from which the temple of Apollo and the imperial palace could be seen simultaneously was called Area Palatina in later antiquity. Plate 48 attempts to reconstruct a general view of it.

Anyone approaching the Area Palatina about the second century A.D.

from the Sacra Via and the Velia would have the temple of Apollo with its annexes on his left, the east side; the palace of Tiberius on his right, and directly in front of him would be the façade of the palace of Augustus, magnificently restored by the Flavian dynasty. In this restoration the level of the palace was elevated more than one story, and while the entrance to the original Domus Augustiana was on the Area itself, the façade of the Flavian palace overtopped it considerably by means of a high projecting terrace (Fig. 27).

We turn now to the other half of the imperial buildings, on the right (west). The palace of Tiberius (Domus Tiberiana) was begun by him during the reign of Augustus while he was heir apparent. At that time it faced the Area Palatina and its back was toward the Velabrum. The proximity of the birthplace of Tiberius may not have been without influence

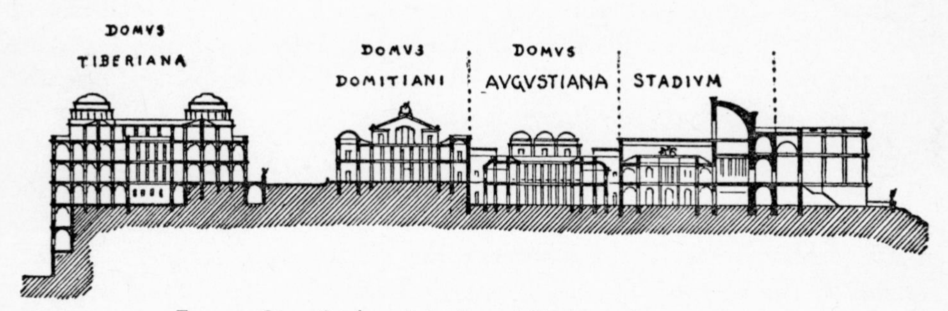

FIG. 27. Cross Section of the Imperial Palaces from W. to E.

on the choice of situation; the south side of the palace almost touches the Domus Liviae, described above. The existing remains date almost exclusively from the alterations in the time of the Antonines (middle of the second century A.D.). Of the general arrangement we can only be sure that the buildings were grouped around three right-angled courts and that the entire area was an oblong 100 × 80 metres in extent. When there was no room left for additional structures on the summit of the hill, at the level of the modern Farnese gardens, the street rising around the northwest corner of the hill (Clivus Victoriae) was bridged over with large arcades and made into a tunnellike passageway in order to provide room on the upper platform thus constructed for an extension of the palace of Tiberius (plate 49). Of the older Domus Tiberiana two stories with vaulted chambers and a porch in front are preserved on the Clivus Victoriae. The remains of the wall decoration in fresco and stucco recall

Pompeian decoration from the last period of that city. From the balcony, recognized as such by the handsome much restored marble balustrade there was, before the arcade was built over the street, a wonderful view extending over the Forum, the Capitol and the City toward the east.

From the façade of the Domus Tiberiana to the Area Palatina the lowest story (cellar) is fairly well preserved; extending along the whole length of the façade from north to south is a vaulted subterranean passage, the cryptoporticus (plate 45, below). Similar subterranean passages were numerous on the Palatine; this extensive network was a necessity for maintaining communication between the various parts of the palace without disturbing the street traffic on the surface of the hill where it was important to leave free access to the temples and shrines which still existed. The cryptoporticus under the façade of the palace of Tiberius was formerly often considered to be the one in which the Emperor Caligula was murdered in 41 A.D. But this is impossible because according to Suetonius the part of the palace in which Caligula met his death was destroyed by fire early in the second century. One thing worthy of note in the story of the murder is that these subterranean passages were intended not only for the servants but were used occasionally also by the rulers. Accordingly many of the passages, as existing remains show, were handsomely decorated: the vaulting in one passage opening at right angles into the cryptoporticus is beautifully embellished with stucco (plate 50).

We go back to the Area Palatina and turn toward the palace of Augustus, which occupies the south side. After Nero's fire it was magnificently restored and enlarged by the three emperors of the Flavian dynasty: Vespasian, Titus and especially Domitian (81–96 A.D.) and is therefore often referred to as the palace of the Flavians (see reconstruction of the whole, plate 52 and Fig. 28). When it was restored the damaged walls of the Augustan building were not demolished, but they were incorporated into the foundations of the new building. The ground floor of the Flavian palace lies one story higher than that of Augustus. Access from the Area is not by a magnificent flight of stairs but merely by modest steps at the side, while in the central portion a high gallery ran along the entire front (plates 51 and 52 and Fig. 29). This striking arrangement is accounted for by explaining that the builder, the suspicious Domitian, desired, when he had to show himself to his assembled subjects on the Area Palatina to do so from a safe place. The façade may have had a colonnade of moderate height on the gallery with sloping roof, above which rose the walls of the side rooms and the high projecting central room. The nearest analogy to this is presented by the façades of the ancient Christian basilicas (S. Maria in Trastevere, S. Lorenzo fuori).

From the portico three doors led into an equal number of large halls. The central one called tablinum or throne room (Aula Regia) has the imposing width of fifty-two metres and the barrel vaulting that covered it was ten metres wider than the central nave of St. Peter's (Fig. 30). A

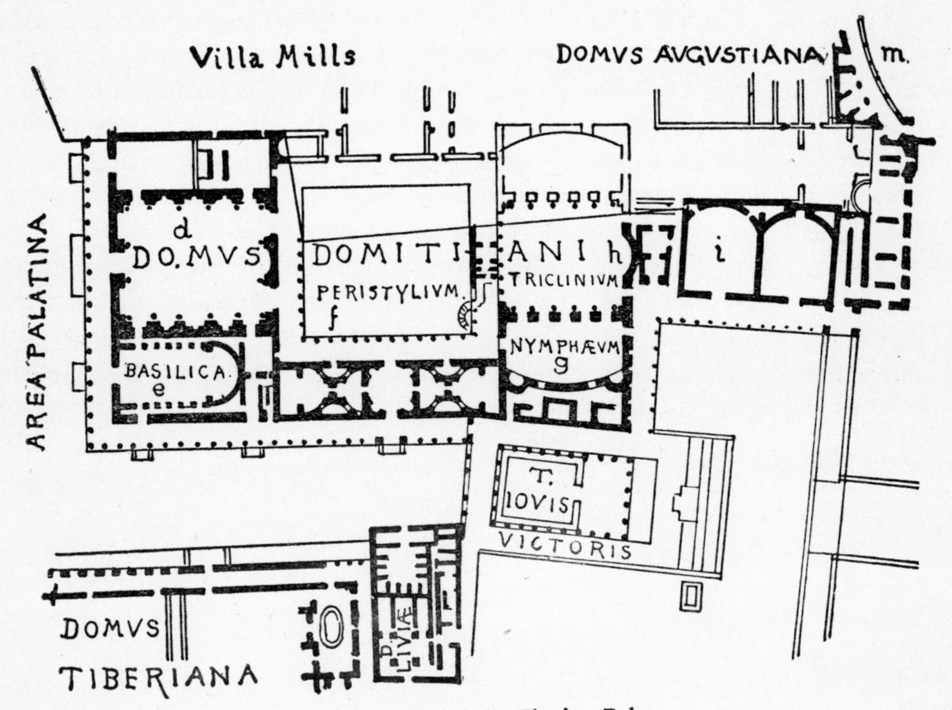

FIG. 28. Plan of the Flavian Palace

flat curved apse opposite the entrance probably marks the place where the imperial throne stood. In the niche a long inscription on a marble tablet recalls the excavations of the Dukes of Parma in the 1720's. There were three niches on the lower part of each of the side walls with a gigantic statue in each. Two such colossuses of basalt, a Hercules and a Bacchus, were found in the course of the excavations in 1726 and are now in the museum at Parma. The black color of the basalt formed a striking contrast to the rich polychrome marble decoration of the niches and the walls: the latter were faced with slabs of white and colored marble, porphyry and serpentine; while the niches were flanked by large columns of giallo antico with richly ornamented entablatures. Only meagre remains are left today of all this splendor: whatever of value was found in the excavations of 1726, whether marble, porphyry, alabaster or other valuable stones, the directors of the enterprise sold to stone masons and mosaic workers by the load to cover the cost of the work.

The most westerly of the three rooms is usually designated as the basilica (plate 54, above) but this is misleading as the use of that word would create the impression that the room had two side aisles and a raised central nave. But it is obvious that no side aisles could have existed here,

FIG. 29. Façade of the Flavian Palace, restored

as the columns—there were two rows, one above the other—were too near the walls, which had a marble facing over the brick core. Rooms such as these, in which the rows of columns merely accompany the wall decoration, so to speak, are often found in palatial Roman houses, among others, the Villa of Hadrian.

The room on the Palatine has always had a uniform roof without any elevation of the central nave; originally this was no doubt a flat wooden ceiling later replaced by a large cross vault. The ceiling was supported by four huge pillars built into the corners, now partly destroyed. This room also had a semicircular apse, opposite the entrance portal, which is separated from the main room by a much restored marble balustrade.

The room adjoining the central room on the east is today quite without decoration. At the time of the excavations of 1725 a pedestal was discovered at the south wall, richly faced with marble, which was explained as being an altar, and so the room itself was called lararium (palace shrine), a name which scarcely suited it.

Behind the so-called lararium a (modern) flight of steps leads down to the remains of the older (Augustan) structures which Domitian's architects incorporated in the foundations of the new palace. These rooms are of modest dimensions with tasteful frescoes somewhat in the style of the House of Livia. Similar rooms beneath the so-called basilica have been excavated, but they are not open to the public.

Behind the so-called throne room and to the south lies a large colonnade (peristylium), the centre of which was probably embellished by a garden. In the centre of it is a labyrinthine brick pavement much restored which is believed to have enclosed flower beds. The surrounding porticoes,

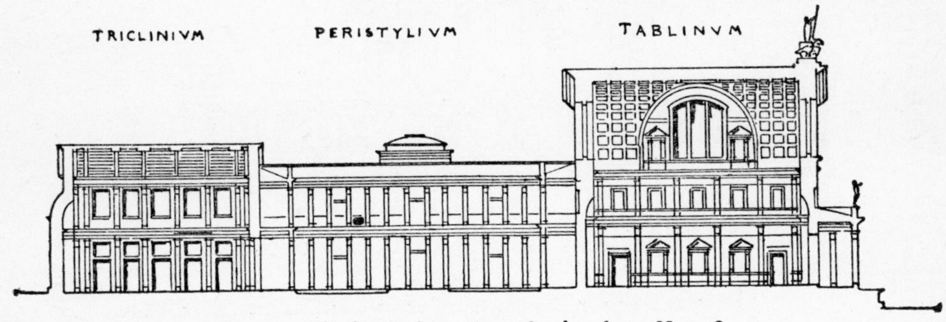

FIG. 30. Flavian Palace, Cross Section from N. to S.

colonnades of costly marble, were probably two stories high. From both the east and the west porticoes one entered three chambers of a baroque plan, divided up by many party walls and niches (see plate 53).

Adjoining the peristyle on the south is a large right-angled room with a flat apse and a chamber at either side of it, connected with the main room by two doors and three large windows. These latter looked out on two fountains of unusual shape: they had elliptical basins with a sort of island built up in the middle cut up by flat and semicircular niches in which one may imagine reliefs and statues (plate 54, below). Water flowed or trickled down from above, over these decorated portions, and the upper surface of the structures was perhaps planted with flowers and plants. Obviously these chambers were merely appendages to the large central room which is called *triclinium* (dining-room), and probably correctly so.

In the apse at the south wall the marble pavement is well preserved, but the execution of the mosaic is careless, as the axis of the pattern does not even correspond with that of the apse and probably the pavement dates from a later restoration. Characteristically different from this are the remains of mosaics in giallo and serpentine with a beautiful foliage pattern which have lately been uncovered between the oval fountains and the curved rear wall. They are only slightly below the Flavian structures, but considerably above the Augustan, and they are therefore ascribed to Nero, who of course included even the imperial palaces on the Palatine in his so-called Golden House. Several other rooms have likewise been found under the triclinium and the southern half of the peristyle lying about a story below the Flavian level. Some of these rooms are beautifully decorated with stucco and marble.

The rear wall of the room with the fountains comes so close to the temple of Jupiter Victor mentioned above that there is only a narrow alley between them. Since there was an open area in front of the temple, those parts of the palace which lie south of the triclinium, between it and the edge of the hill, are somewhat withdrawn toward the east. Here we find two rooms (Fig. 28 i) with flat apses facing west having a narrow balcony with a portico at the front. The row of columns nearest the triclinium are partly restored: they have shafts of green cipollino with Corinthian capitals of white marble (plates 55 and 56, above). These rooms are called, but without any reason, Academy and Library.

The declivity of the hill to the south of the three rooms is still covered with rubbish; half way up stands a building of a peculiar plan (plate 56, below) oriented according to the imperial palaces and belonging to them. This building consists principally of an elongated court with a colonnade along the north side; several rooms and chambers adjoin the colonnade, of which the rear room abuts directly on the hill. The walls are plastered with simple patterns of no especially artistic value; and many names and inscriptions in Latin and in Greek are scratched into the plaster. Since the word "paedagogium" occurs in several of these scribbled inscriptions, the building has been explained as an annex of the training school for the imperial pages on the Caelian (paedagogium puerorum a caput Africae), though the general impression is not that of a dwelling. More probably it belonged to the rooms for the imperial wardrobe, as other graffiti would lead us to suppose. Among the graffiti found here the so-called caricature of the Crucifixion has aroused especial attention. It is the picture of a man with an ass's head on the cross being adored by a believer with the legend: "Alexamenos worships his god." It is supposed that a pagan slave was mocking a Christian comrade by means of this picture.

With the exception of this last building the part of the palace described thus far consists exclusively of magnificent large rooms for assemblies; the imperial living quarters lay in the adjoining part on the right, the territory of the former Villa Mills.

Considerable remains were uncovered here in the 1770's and again lately, abutting on the triclinium and the rooms with apses: these comprised numerous rooms and chambers mostly of moderate dimensions, grouped around a square court. Towards the side overlooking the valley of the Circus lay a façade in the shape of a flat arched exedra. On the opposite (north) side we enter three vaulted rooms, the middle one square, those at the sides octagonal. There is scarcely anything left of the beautiful marble facing of the walls which was still in a very complete state of preservation at the time of the excavations in the 18th century. The rear wall of the three vaulted rooms abuts on the hill, and it formed the end of the lower story, while the upper story extended northward for a considerable distance.

Remains which were found lying within the casino and the garden of the Villa Mills, as well as reports of excavations in the 16th century, and some fragments of Severus' marble plan of the City prove that this part of the palace was composed throughout of rooms of small dimensions. On some of the brick walls within the Villa Mills there are much damaged remains of early mediaeval frescoes—they are identified as belonging to the monastery of S. Cesareo (see p. 74, below).

East of the palace and closely connected with the living rooms in the upper story, is a building which is distinguished by its excellent state of preservation (plate 57). This is an elongated court ending in a curve at the south side and surrounded by high walls which were originally perhaps accompanied only by simple colonnades; at the north end was a balcony at the level of the upper story of the palace. The first annex dates perhaps from the time of Domitian; while under Hadrian it was enlarged by the addition of a high semicircular exedra with hemispherical vaulting built in the centre of the east side. Then the arcade resting on stout pillars with engaged columns which surrounds the entire lower area dates from the time of Septimius Severus. The upper platform of it was likewise at the level of the first story of the palace, and it was accessible from the living quarters through several large doors. Since the 18th century this building has been called Hippodromus Palatii (Palatine Hippodrome), a name taken from the Acts of Saint Sebastian the martyr, who was venerated at a very early date in the neighboring church of S. Maria in Pallara. The ground plan of this building which was buried in rubbish, seemed well suited for its use as a race course. But when, after 1870, the excavations were extended down to the ancient level, the remains of two large richly decorated fountains were discovered at the north and south ends and also in the centre, foundations of bases and pedestals which, it is safe to conclude, were richly ornamented with works of art. The basins of the fountains are so short a distance from the surrounding porticoes that it is out of the question to have used this space for chariot or horse races. But since it was desirable to continue to call this building by a name connected with athletics, it was called *Stadium,* which means a track for foot races, although there is no known mention of a stadium within the palaces of the Caesars and indeed it is extremely unlikely that any such existed there. The correct explanation and name were only recently arrived at by the observation that *Hippodromus* in Roman architecture means not only a race course but also an elongated garden in the form of one. And so we must imagine the lower portion with flower beds and lawns and hanging gardens set on the encircling colonnade with its heavy arches. In plate 58 an attempt is made to give a picture of the whole in antiquity.

The elliptical structure in the southern half of the building dates from a very late period, as is proved by the bricks found in its walls stamped with the names of the Gothic kings Theodoric (483–526) and Athalaric (526–532). As the cornerstone of the southern entrance a pedestal with an honorary inscription to the Vestal Coelia Claudiana (about 290 A.D.) was used, which could, naturally, not have been removed from the Atrium Vestae until the latter was abandoned (382 A.D.). Lately, for some inexplicable reason the stone was moved back to the House of the Vestals. The purpose of the elliptical structure is uncertain, it may have been an enclosure for wild beasts. Since the beginning of the ninth century A.D. a church has stood in the centre of the Hippodrome dedicated to Saint Caesarius, with a monastery for Greek monks. The latter was considered for a long time to be one of the most distinguished abbeys in Rome, and the buildings extended, it would seem, as far as the territory of the Villa Mills. In the 14th century it was in ruins and is not mentioned after the beginning of the 15th century.

At the north end of the Hippodrome, accessible from the balcony frequently mentioned above, lies a large square room with semicircular niches which was for a long time erroneously supposed to be one of the rooms of the library of Augustus. But when it was completely excavated remains of basins were found in the niches so that it may be that the room should rather be considered a magnificent *Nymphaeum*. Other rooms and halls to the west were excavated in the 16th century in the garden of the Villa Mills, but were again covered up.

The northern boundary of all of these structures is a continuation of the façade of the palace of the Flavians, another proof that the entire area lying between the Nymphaeum and the three large halls belonged to the palace.

Various living rooms which originally extended to the edge of the hill over the Circus Maximus abut on the east side of the Hippodrome to the south of the large exedra. A bathing establishment, which, according to the brick stamps, dates from the time of Hadrian, is one of the groups easily recognized. This whole wing of the imperial palaces was built over toward the end of the second century by new structures under Septimius Severus (193–211).

A street probably ran in early times from the south corner of the hill down into the valley between the Palatine and the Caelian, and Severus bridged it over with great arcades as in the case of the Clivus Victoriae (see above) in order to gain room on the heights for a new wing of the palace (plate 59). The ground floor of this building of Severus corresponded to the level of the upper story of the Domus Augustiana: we can see by the ruins of the lofty stairway (plate 60) that this was an imposing structure. The adjoining ruins are the foundation walls of a great hall (triclinium?) which opens far out to the east and must have presented a wonderful view of the southern quarters of the City and of the Campagna as far as the Alban hills, similar to the view one may now enjoy from the end of the portico, the so-called Belvedere of the palace of Severus (plate 61).

There was a monument not directly connected with the palace of Severus, but inseparable from it historically, the Septizonium. This rose only a short distance away from the ruins at the foot of the hill, described above, and until the end of the 16th century it was among the most conspicuous and best known of Rome's ruins. It was built by Severus, the first African to occupy the imperial Roman throne, in order, as his biographer has it (in Scriptores Historiae Augustae) "that when his compatriots came up from Africa a monument to him might at once strike their eyes."

This building formed the perspective view for the Via Appia which had its terminus here. It was merely a showy three-story façade with colonnades of white and colored marble without any rooms for domestic or religious purposes behind it. In front of the façade lay a large basin into which streams of water poured from three niches in the façade. The effect must have been similar to that of the Fountain of Trevi in a threefold repetition. Even at the close of the eighth century and the beginning of the ninth, the structure still stood in almost perfect condition; later it served Roman nobles as a fortification and a branch of the Frangipani family used the epithet de Septisolio in the 12th and 13th centuries. About this time it was already in ruins except for the right (north) corner. In the 15th and 16th centuries architects very industriously studied these remains, and plate 62 gives an idea of its appearance as shown in drawings made by Martin van Heemskerck.

As its decay continued, Sextus V had it torn down in 1586, so that today no part of the building is to be seen above ground. The foundations which must still be in place underground and which would be interesting for our knowledge of this unique structure, were unfortunately not investigated at the time of the laying out of the new *Passeggiata Archeologica,* but were covered up even deeper than before and probably forever buried.

DESTRUCTION AND EXCAVATION OF THE IMPERIAL PALACES

WITH the transfer of the imperial residence from Rome to Byzantium the decay of the buildings on the Palatine also began. It is true that the rulers of the western Roman Empire still frequently dwelt on the Palatine down to the end of the Empire (476 A.D.), and even after the fall of the imperial power, Theodoric (483–526) the great king of the Goths took pains to see that the buildings were kept in repair. As late as the year 570 the Byzantine Governor Narses lived in the palace, and the short chronicle which reports this fact alone adds that he had "the statues" removed from the palace, in order, presumably, to drag off to Byzantium the works of art he stole.

For more than a century thereafter the history of the Palatine is completely obscured, though recent scholars have assumed that as early as 600 a chapel to Saint Caesarius existed within the deserted palace, and that the Byzantine emperor Heraclius had himself crowned on the Palatine in 629, but neither assumption will bear close examination.

Reliable sources of information are wanting till the beginning of the eighth century. We are told that Pope John VII, the son of Plato, the Byzantine major domo of the palace (Curopalata), built himself a bishop's palace (Episcopium) near the north corner, above the church of S. Maria Antiqua, that is, within the territory of the Domus Tiberiana. The Christian religion had not at this time established itself on the summit of the hill, though it had begun to do so on the slope. The church of S. Anastasia below the west corner was standing as early as the fourth century; S. Maria Antiqua and the round church of Saint Theodore date from the sixth century; and the church of Saint Lucia beside the Septizonium, from the eighth century.

Greek monks settled on the summit of the hill at the beginning of the ninth century; their monastery nestled in the deserted rooms of the Domus Augustiana and their church, dedicated to Saint Caesarius, stood in the centre of the Hippodrome.

A second monastery, founded by Latin monks, arose not long before the year 1000 on the east corner, in the precinct of the temple of Apollo. It bore the name of S. Maria in Pallara or in Palladio, and besides the Virgin, Saints Zoticus and Sebastian were worshipped there. The latter, according to the legend, died a martyr's death in the Hippodrome near-by. The monastery of S. Maria in Pallara appears frequently in the 12th century, during the incessant feuds of the nobles, as a place of refuge for the popes. "The safest place in the city, which belongs to the Papal Court," a contemporary chronicler calls it. The papal archives were for a long time kept in the Torre Cartularia, between the so-called Pallara and the arch of Titus. But the greater part of the Palatine was in those centuries a labyrinth of ruins, covered with meagre vineyards and gardens, a large part of the hill belonged to the Frangipani family. The author of the Mirabilia (about 1150) who wove such detailed romances about the Forum, makes short work of the Palatine in his little book. In the descriptions of the City of the 15th century and the beginning of the 16th century it is expressly stated that none of the seven hills is so deserted as the Palatine. The monasteries of S. Cesareo and S. Maria in Pallara were also abandoned after the middle of the 15th century, though the latter was later restored.

Under the pontificate of Paul III (1534–1549) the nephew of the Pope Cardinal Alessandro Farnese bought up numerous vineyards and gardens and united the western and the central parts of the hill into one large continuous domain. Under the direction of Vignola a magnificent garden developed here with an entrance at the north opposite the basilica of Constantine. Magnificent terraces led up to the plateau at the summit, which was ornamented with hedges and flower beds and oak groves and fountains; there was no extensive villa with huge rooms, but numerous graceful little pavilions and arbors were scattered around. Engravings and drawings from the 16th to the 19th centuries give us an idea of this much admired creation of the cardinal (see plates 63, 64). After his death the entire estate went to his relatives, the Dukes of Parma, in whose possession it remained until 1731. The Palatine was practically untouched by excavation throughout the whole of the 17th century and it was not until the latter part of their ownership, beween 1720 and 1730 that the Dukes of Parma began extensive excavations in the central part of the ruins, in the three large halls of the palace of the Flavians. These excavations purposed not so much a scientific investigation of the remains as discoveries of works of art and costly marble. The finds went partly to Parma and partly by inheritance to Naples. The learned Francesco Bianchini planned a scientific revision of them, but he died before he could finish his work, and his preliminary studies fell into the hands of incompetent and conscienceless compilers, so that the folio volume which appeared under his name, Del Palazzo dei Cesari (1728), was merely productive of confusion and served no useful purpose.

The villa which abuts on the Farnese gardens on the east, and which belonged to the Mattei family in the 17th century, came into the possession of the Abbé Rancoureuil, a Frenchman, in 1770. He instituted thoroughgoing excavations in the following decade which led to the discovery of a part of the Domus Augustiana. This same villa came into the possession of Charles Mills, an Englishman, at the beginning of the 19th century and he covered over the casino with the extraordinary false Gothic veneer which is today * still conspicuous in the midst of the classical remains.

Investigation of the ruins was interrupted until in 1861 Emperor Napoleon III bought the Farnese gardens in order to undertake systematic excavations.

The Roman architect Pietro Rosa, to whom the direction of the work had been entrusted, uncovered the northern and central parts of the palaces of Tiberius and the Flavians in the course of the following decade. Of special importance was the discovery of the so-called House of Livia with its wealth of frescoes (1869). After 1871 the Italian Government continued the excavations and extended the work to the east side where it ceased with the partial uncovering of the so-called Stadium (1877–78). After an interval of fifteen years these excavations were continued and finished in 1893; at the same time the vineyard of S. Bonaventura, which abuts on the north, was explored. The east corner with the church of S. Maria in Pallara (now commonly known as S. Sebastiano alla Polveriera) and the Villa Mills, which lies in the centre of the plateau on the summit of the hill, remained unexcavated. The latter was acquired by the Italian Government in 1905, the excavations of 1770 were again made accessible and some of the modern buildings were demolished. On the other hand the

*** As this book goes to press the Author writes to say that within the past few months this Gothic veneer has been almost entirely removed.**

remains between the Hippodrome and the three large halls of the palace of the Flavians, which were entirely unknown, are still intact.

Excavations under the three halls were undertaken in 1911 and the years following, under the direction of Giacomo Boni, which brought to light interesting remains of structures from pre-Flavian days. These structures had been in part reached by the excavations of 1720 but had again been buried. These remains, which are interesting because of their artistic decoration are unfortunately not yet accessible to the public.

SOURCES AND RECENT LITERATURE

In the following bibliography attention has been paid principally to the more recent publications. For the older literature the reader is referred to the sections in Jordan-Huelsen, *Topographie* (Forum: vol. I, 2, pp. 195–429; Palatine: vol. I, p. 3, 29–111): for this reason an exact citation of it has been given in every case. In addition references have been given to R. A. Lanciani, *Ruins and Excavations of Ancient Rome* (London, 1897), to S. B. Platner, *Topography and Monuments of Ancient Rome* (2nd edition, Boston, 1911), and to Tenney Frank, *Roman Buildings of the Republic* (Papers and Monographs of the American Academy in Rome, III, 1924). On the contrary, it will be sufficient to refer once and for all to some serviceable monographs: A. Bartoli, *Il Foro Romano; Il Palatino,* Roma, s. a. (1924); O. Marucchi, *Le Forum Romain et le Palatin* (Paris and Rome, 1902); G. Lugli, *La Zona archeologica di Roma* (Roma, 1924, deals with the Forum on pp. 52–112, with the Palatine, pp. 159–221). For the Forum especially: H. Thédenat, *Le Forum Romain et les Forums Impériaux* (3rd ed., Paris, 1904); Mrs. E. Burton-Brown, *Recent Excavations in the Roman Forum* (London, 1904); W. St. Clair Baddeley, *Recent Discoveries in the Roman Forum* (London, 1904); D. Vaglieri, *Gli scavi recenti nel Foro Romano* (reprint from the Bullettino archeologico comunale, 1903, pp. 3–239, 252–275); my own little book, *The Roman Forum, Its History and Its Monuments,* translated by Jesse Benedict Carter (2nd ed., Rome, 1909; *Nachtrag,* only in German, Rome, 1911), is quoted rarely; instead, I have occasionally referred to my *Berichte über die Forums-Ausgrabungen* (Röm. Mitteilungen, 1902, pp. 3–97; 1905, 1–119). For the Palatine, I mention the monograph of Count Eberhard Haugwitz, *Der Palatin, seine Geschichte und seine Ruinen* (Rome, 1901). Finally, inasmuch as not every classical philologist and historian has access to the Corpus Inscriptionum Latinarum, as far as possible the numbers of the inscriptions in Orelli Henzen and H. Dessau, *Inscriptiones selectæ,* have been added.

(P. 1.) The Sepulcretum at the Velia.

Boni, *Notizie degli scavi,* 1902, 96–111; 1903, 123–170; 375–427; 1905, 145–193; 1906, 5–46; 253–294; 1911, 157–190. Huelsen, *Röm. Mitt.,* 1902, 92–94; 1905, 95–115. Pinza, *Monumenti dei Lincei* XV (1905), 273–314. Platner, 187f. v. Duhn, *Italische Gräberkunde,* I (1924), 417–431; 458–467.

(P. 2.) The Sepulcretum Near the Volcanal.

v. Duhn, *Neue Heidelberger Jahrbücher* IX (1899), 113–115; *Italische Gräberkunde,* 414f.

THE FORUM AND THE PALATINE

(P. 2.) The Niger Lapis and the Grave of Romulus.

Festus, p. 177. Dionysius, I, 87; III, 1. Schol. Horat. on *Epod.,* 16; 13, 14.

(P. 4.) The Inscription on the Cippus.

Dessau, 4913. Huelsen, *Klio* II (1902), 230. Warren, *American Journal of Philology,* 1907, 249, 373. Kretschmer, *Wiener Studien,* 1904, 158. CIL. I^2 p. 367, n. 1.

Jordan I, 2, 356. Boni, *Not. de scavi,* 1899, 151–169, 1900. Savignoni, ib. 1900, 143–146. Huelsen, *Röm. Mitt.,* 1902, 22–31; 1905, 40–46. Studniczka, *Jahreshefte des Oesterr. Instituts* VI (1903) 129–155; VII (1904), 239f. Petersen, *Comitium, Rostra, Grab des Romulus* (Rom 1904). Platner, 241–250. Van Deman, *Journal of Roman Studies,* 1922, 23–25. v. Duhn, *Italische Gräberkunde,* I (1924), 415f. Frank, 61f.

(P. 5.) The Tullianum and the Carcer.

Varro, *L. L.,* V, 150. Festus, 264, 346. Sallust, *Catilin.,* 55. Livius, I, 33, 8; III, 57, 6; XXIX, 22, 10; XXXIV, 44, 8. Velleius, II, 72. Valer. Max., IX, 12, 6. Plin., *n.h.* VII, 212. Seneca, *controv.* IX, 27, 20. Calpurnius Flaccus, *decl.* 4. Ammianus Marcellin., XXVIII, 1, 57. Servius, *ad Aen.* VI, 573. CIL. VI, 1539.

Jordan, I, 1, 435; I, 2, 323–328. Gori-de Mauro-Parker, *Ichnographia teterrimi carceris Mamertini* (Rome, 1868; reprint from *Il Buonarroti,* vol. III). Duchesne, *Le Forum Chrétien,* 19–32. Pinza, *Rendiconti dei Lincei,* 1902, 226–239. Platner, 250–252. Frank, 39–47. Huelsen, *Chiese di Roma,* 421, 19.

(P. 7.) Cloaca Maxima.

Livius, I, 38, 6; 56, 2. Dionys., III, 67, 2; IV, 44, 1. Llinius, *n.h.* XXXVI 164. Servius, *ad Aen.* XII, 603. Auctor *de viris illustr.,* 8, 3. Georgius Codinus, I, p. 260, ed. Bonn. CIL, VI, 7882 (= Dessau 7719).

Jordan, I, 1, 441–443, 447–452. Richter, *Antike Denkmäler,* I, pl. 37. Narducci, *fognatura di Roma,* 39–49. Platner, 107–109, 271f. Frank, 74, 142.

(P. 10.) Tabernae Veteres, Novae, Argentariae.

Plautus, *Curculio* IV, 1, 19. Varro, *ap. Nonium,* 532, 1, 1; VI, 59. Cicero, *Acad. prior* II, 70; *de oratore,* II, 266. Livius, I, 35; XXVI, 27, 2; XL, 51, 5; XLIV, 16, 10. Dionys., III, 67. Plinius, *n.h.* XXXV, 26; 113. Festus, 230.

Jordan, I, 2, 379f. Platner, 168f.

(P. 10.) Columna Maenia.

Cicero, *in Verr. divin.,* 16, 50. Ascon, p. 123, Orelli. Schol. Bobiens. *ad. Cicer. pro Sestio,* 15 p. 295, Orelli. Plinius, *n.h.* VII, 212; XXXIV, 20. Plutarch, *Cato*

minor, 5. Paulus ex Festo, 134. Porphyrio *in Horat. sat.* I, 3, 21. Symmachus, *ep.* V, 54, 3.
Jordan, I, 2, 345. Huelsen, *Röm. Mitt.,* 1893, 84, 92. Platner, 169, 231f.

(P. 10.) COLUMNA ROSTRATA OF DUILIUS.

CIL. I, 195=VI, 1300 (=Dessau, 65). Plinius, *n.h.* XXXIV, 20. Quintilian, *inst. or.* I, 7, 12. Servius, *ad Georg.* III, 29.
Jordan, I, 2, 231. Wölfflin, *Münchener Sitz. Ber.,* 1890, 290–321. Lanciani, *R. and E.,* 256; *stor. d. scavi,* II, 188. Platner, 220.

(P. 10.) STATUES IN THE FORUM.

Plinius, *n.h.* XXXIV, 30.
Jordan, I, 2, 401.

(P. 10.) BASILICA PORCIA.

Livius, XXXIX, 44. Ascon., *ad Cicer. in Milonem,* p. 29, ed. Orelli. Plutarch, *Cato maior,* 19; *Cato minor,* 5. Auctor *de viris illustr.* 47. SC. de Oropiis (a. 681), ap. Bruns, *Fontes iuris romani,*[5] 162.
Jordan, I, 2, 344. Huelsen, *Röm. Mitt.,* 1893, 84. Platner, 230.

(P. 11.) BASILICA SEMPRONIA.

Livius, XLIV, 16.
Jordan, I, 2, 384. Platner, 192.

(P. 11.) BASILICA OPIMIA.

Varro, *L. L.,* V, 155. Cicero, *pro Sestio,* 67, 140. CIL. I, 1067, 1068; VI, 2338, 2339 (=Dessau, 1969).
Jordan, I, 2, 338, 384. Huelsen, *Röm. Mitt.,* 1893, 84. Platner, 174.

(P. 14.) TEMPLUM DIVI IULII.

Monum. Ancyr., IV, 2. Ovid, *met.* XV, 841; *ex ponto* II, 2, 85. Vitruv., III, 2, 2. Appian, *b.c.* I, 4, II, 148. Plinius, *n.h.* XXXV, 27, 91. Statius, *silv.* I, i, 22. Cassius Dio, XLVII, 18, 4, 19, 2; LI, 19, 2, 22, 2. Hemerol. Antiat. Allif. ad XV kal. Sept. Acta Arval. a. 69 Febr., 26 (CIL. VI, 2051, 55). Coins: Cohen,[2] Auguste, 89; Hadrien, 416–419, 388.
Jordan, I, 2, 406–409. Richter, *Jahrbuch des Instituts,* 1889, 137–162. Antike Denkmäler, I, pl. 27, 28. Lanciani, *R. and E.,* 269; *storia d. scavi II,* 197. Platner, 183. Fiechter-Toebelmann, *Gebälke* I, 8; *Zeitschrift für Gesch. der Architektur* VIII (1924), 62–72.

THE FORUM AND THE PALATINE

(P. 15.) ARCUS AUGUSTI.

Cassius Dio, LIV, 8. Scholia Veron, *Vergil,* p. 98. Coin: Cohen,[2] Auguste, 82–85.

Jordan, I, 2, 211. Richter, *Jahrbuch des Instituts,* 1889, 151–162. Antike Denkmäler, I, Taf. 27, 28. Lanciani, *R. and E.,* 270. Curtis, *Suppl. Papers Amer. School in Rome,* II, 48. Platner, 253. Fiechter-Toebelmann, *Gebälke* I, 13–26.

(P. 15.) BASILICA IULIA.

Cicero, *ad Att.,* IV, 16. Mon. Ancyr., IV, 13. Martial, VI, 38, 6. Paulus ex Festo, 290. Statius, *silv.,* I, 1, 29. Sueton., *Aug.,* 29; *Cal.,* 37. Plinius *ep.* V, 9 (21), VI, 33. Quintilian XII, 5, 6. Cassius Dio, LVI, 27; LXVIII, 10. Schol. Juvenal., 4, 81. Notitia, reg. VIII et app. Chronogr., a. 354, p. 145. Momms., FUR. fr. 20, 23. CIL. VI, 1658, 9709 (Dessau, 7509), 9711 (=Henzen 5082), 9712, 10040, 10042, 31883–31887 (=Dessau, 5537).

Jordan, I, 2, 385–391. Lanciani, *R. and E.,* 275–279; *storia d. scavi,* II, 205f. Rivoira, *Origini dell' Architettura Lombarda,* II, 488, 489. Platner, 192f. Frank, 76. Huelsen, *Chiese di Roma nel Medio evo* (1927), p. 321, n. 25.

(P. 18.) ARCUS TIBERII.

Tacit., *ann.* II, 41. CIL. VI, 906, 31422, 31575.

Montiroli, *Osservazioni sul Foro Romano* (1849), 12. Jordan, I, 2, 212, 410. Mommsen, *Res. gestae Divi Augusti,*[2] 126. Lanciani, *R. and E.,* 284. Curtis, *Suppl. Papers Amer. School in Rome,* II, 47. Platner, 254.

(P. 18.) MILLIARIUM AUREUM.

Plinius, *n.h.* III, 66. Tacitus, *hist.* I, 27. Sueton., *Otho* 6. Plutarch, *Galba,* 24. Cassius Dio, LIV, 8. Notit., reg. VIII.

Jordan, I, 2, 24. Richter, *römische Rednerbühne,* 35–37. Lanciani, *R. and E.,* 281. Platner, 226.

(P. 18.) THE SO-CALLED ROSTRA CAESARIS.

Not. degli scavi 1899, 627–634. Huelsen, *Röm. Mitt.,* 1902, 15; *Forum,* 70. Platner, 227f.

(P. 18.) TEMPLUM SATURNI.

Varro, *L. L.,* V, 41. Livius, II, 21, 1; XXII, 1, 19; XLI, 21, 12; 27, 7. Dionys. 1, 34; VI, 1, 4. Festus, 322. Sueton., *August,* 29. Tacitus, *ann. II,* 41. Plutarch, *qu. Rom.* 42; Ti. Gracchus, 10. Appian., *bell. civ.* I, 31. Macrobius, *sat.* I, 8. Servius, *ad Aen.* II, 216; VIII, 319. FUR. fr. 22, 23, 30. CIL. VI, 937, 1316 (=Dessau 41); X, 6087 (=Dessau 886). Hemerol., Antiat. *Not. d. scavi,* 1921, 119 et Amitern. ad XIV kal. Jan.

Jordan, I, 2, 360–363. Lanciani, *R. and E.*, 293. Platner, 178. Toebelmann-Fiechter, *Gebälke*, 7, 65.

(P. 20.) PORTICUS DEORUM CONSENTIUM.

CIL. VI, 102, 30692 (=Dessau 4003). Varro, *de re rust.* I, 4.

Jordan, I, 2, 192, 367, 411. Lanciani, *R. and E.*, 291–294. Platner, 177f. Van Deman, *American Journal of Archaeology*, 1912, 411, 414. Frank, 55f.

(P. 20.) TEMPLUM DIVI VESPASIANI.

CIL. VI, 938 (=Dessau 255), 1019 (=Dessau 382). Notita, reg. VIII. Chronogr. a. 354, p. 146, Momms.

Jordan, I, 2, 192, 411. Lanciani, *R. and E.*, 291. Platner, 176.

(P. 21.) TEMPLUM CONCORDIAE.

Varro, *L. L.*, V, 148. Plutarch, *Camill.*, 42; *C. Gracchus*, 17. Ovid, *fast* I, 637. Appian, *b. civ.* I, 26. Statius, *silv.* I, 1, 30. Sueton., *Tib.*, 20. Cassius Dio LV, 82; LVI, 25, 1; LVIII, 11. Augustinus, *de civ. dei* III, 24. CIL. VI, 89 (=Dessau 3781); 90 (=Dessau 3782); 91–94; 3675, 30856 (=Dessau 3783). Hemerol. Praenest. ad XVII kal. Febr.; hemerol. Pincian. et Antiat, *Not. d. scavi* 1921, 103 ad XI kal. Sextil. Acta Arvalium, passim. Coin of Orbiana in Froehner, *Médaillons*, p. 157. FUR. fr., 22.

Dutert, *Le Forum*, p. 35 and pl. XIV. Jordan, I, 2, 332–336. Lanciani, *R. and E.*, 288. Van Buren, *Classical Review*, 1906, 82–84. Platner, 174f. Mancini, *Not. d. scavi* 1921 l. c. Fiechter-Toebelmann, *Gebälke*, 42–51. Rebert and Marceau, *Memoirs of the American Academy in Rome*, V (1925).

(P. 21.) ARCUS SEVERI.

CIL. VI, 1033 (=Dessau, 425). Coins of Severus: Cohen², Severus, 53, 104. Caracalla, 14, 15.

Rossini, *Archi trionfali tav.* 50–59. Jordan, I, 2, 213. Lanciani, *R. and E.*, 284. Curtis, *Suppl. Papers Americ. School*, II, 47. Platner, 254f.

(P. 22.) UMBILICUS URBIS ROMAE.

Notit. reg. VIII. Anonymus Einsidlensis in Jordan II, 655.

Jordan, I, 2, 245. Lanciani, *R. and E.*, 282. Huelsen, *Atti dell'Accad. Pontificia*, ser. II, vol. VI, p. 389. Platner, 226.

(P. 22.) VOLCANAL.

Livius IX, 46, 6; XXXIX, 46; XL, 19, 2. Dionys. II, 50, 2; VI, 67, 2; VII, 17, 2; XI, 39, 1. Plinius, *n.h.* XVI 236. Gellius IV, 5. Festus, 238, 290. Plutarch,

Popl., 16. Auctor, *de vir. ill.,* 11, 2. Hemerol. Arval. et Antiat. *Not. d. scavi* 1921, p. 109. CIL. VI, 457 (=Dessau, 93).

Jordan, I, 2, 339. Lanciani, *bull. comun.* 1902, 125–133. Huelsen, *Röm. Mitt.,* 1905, 5–7. Platner, 173. Mancini, *Not. d. scavi* 1921 l. c., v. Duhn, *Italische Gräberkunde,* I, 415.

(P. 22.) ROSTRA OF AUGUSTUS.

Seneca, *dial.* II, 1, 3. Sueton., *Aug.,* 100; Fronto, *ad Antonin.* I, 2, p. 98, Naber. Cassius Dio, XLIII, 49; LVI, 34; LXXIV, 3. Pompon., *de origine iuris,* Dig. I, 2, 2, Mamertinus, genethl. Maximian., 19. Prudentius, *peristeph.* XI, 45. Aur. Victor, *epit.* 19. Reliefs of the arch of Constantine: Canina, *edif.* II, tav. 91.

Jordan, I, 2, 233, 314. Richter, *Röm. Rednerbühne* 8–39; *Jahrbuch des Instituts,* 1889, 1–17; *Beiträge zur römischen Topographie* II (1903). Lanciani, *R. and E.,* 280. Mau, *Röm. Mitt.* 1905, 230–266. Petersen, ib. 1906, 57–63. Van Deman, *American Journal of Archaeol.,* 1909, 170–186. Platner, 220–226.

(P. 24.) THE SO-CALLED ANAGLYPHA OF TRAJAN.

Brizio, *Annali dell' Instituto,* 1872, 309. Monumenti dell' Inst. IX tav. 47, 48. Henzen, *Bullettino dell' Inst.,* 1872, 273–281. Jordan, I, 2, 219–226. Lanciani, *R. and E.,* 256f. Petersen, *Festschrift für A. v. Oettingen* (1890), 130–143. A. S. Jenkins, *American Journal of Archaeology,* 1901, 58–82. Huelsen, *Röm. Mitt.,* 1902, 21. Platner, 263–266. Cantarelli, *Bull. arch. comun.*

(P. 27.) TRIBUNAL PRAETORIUM.

Livius, XXVII, 50, 9. Porphyr., *ad Horat., epod.* I, 19, 8. CIL. VI, 1467.

Mommsen, *Juristische Schriften* III (1907), 319–326. Jordan, I, 2, 402. Huelsen, *Forum, Nachtrag* (1910), 16–21. Platner, 269.

(P. 27.) STATUA MARSYAE.

Horat., *sat.* I, 6, 120. Seneca, *de benef.* 6, 32. Plin., *n.h.* XXI, 8, 9. Martial, II, 64, 7. Servius, *ad Aen.* III, 20. Ps.-Acron et Porphyr. *ad Horat.* l. c. Coins: Cohen-Babelon,[2] Marcia 42.

Jordan, I, 2, 265. Huelsen, *Forum, Nachtrag,* 19. Platner, 269. A Reinach, *Klio,* 1914, 321–337.

(P. 28.) LACUS CURTIUS.

Plautus, *Curculio* IV, 1, 16. Varro, *L. L.,* V, 148. Livius, I, 12, 9; 13, 15; VII, 6, 5. Ovid, *fast.,* VI, 403. Dionys., II, 42, 6. Plinius, *n.h.* XV, 77. Sueton., *August,* 57; *Galba,* 20 Tacit., *hist.* I, 41. Plutarch, *Romul.* 18; *Galba,* 27. Paulus ex Festo, 49. Cassius Dio, fr. 30, 1. Aurel. Victor, *Caes.,* 6, 3; Zonaras, VII, 25. Suidas, s. v. Λίβερνος.

Jordan, I, 2, 399. Huelsen, in *Pauly-Wissowa Real-Encyklopaedie* IV, 1892;

Forum [2] 144 and *Nachtrag* 13. Platner, 267. Van Deman, *Journal of Roman Studies* XII, 8; 20, 21. Frank, 76.

(P. 28.) COLUMNA FOCAE.

CIL. VI, 1200 (=Dessau, 837).
Jordan, I, 2, 246. Lanciani, *R. and E.,* 262. Platner, 260.

(P. 29.) THE OLD ROSTRA.

Varro, *L. L.,* V, 155. Livius IV, 17, 6; VIII, 14, 12. Diodor., XII, 26. Dionys., I, 87. Plinius, *n.h.* VII, 212; XXXIV, 20, 25. Ascon. *in Milon.,* 12. Coin of Palikanus: Cohen-Babelon,[2] Lollia n. 2.
Jordan, I, 2, 353. Huelsen, *Röm. Mitt.* 1905, 29–39; *Forum Nachtrag* 10. Petersen, *Comitium, Rostra, Grab des Romulus* (Rome, 1904). Platner, 220. Frank, 62f.

(P. 29.) COMITIUM.

Passim; especially Plautus, *Curculio* IV, 1, 9. Varro, *L. L.,* V, 155. Cicero, *de rep.* II, 31. Livius, V, 45; XXVII, 36, 8; XXXIV, 45; XL, 29, 14. Plinius *n.h.* X, 5. Sueton, *Octavian,* 43.
Jordan, I, 2, 201–205; 318–322. Huelsen, *Röm. Mitt.* 1893, 79–94; 1902, 32–39. Petersen, *Comitium, Rostra, Grab des Romulus* (Rome, 1904); *Röm. Mitt.,* 1906, 193–210. Platner, 228–232. Frank, 61f.

(P. 30.) CURIA HOSTILIA.

Varro, *L. L.,* V, 154; id. ap. Gellium XIV, 7, 7. Cicero, *pro Milone,* 33. Asconius, *in Milon.,* 33, p. 29, ed. Orelli. Cicero, *de finibus,* V, 1. Livius, I, 30. Plinius, *n.h.* XXXIV, 26. Cassius Dio, XL, 49. CIL. VI, 30207.
Jordan, I, 2, 328–332. Huelsen, *Röm. Mitt.* 1893, 86–91. Lanciani, *R. and E.,* 263. Platner, 229.

(P. 30.) CURIA IULIA.

Monum. Ancyr., IV, 1; VI, 13. Plin. *n.h.* XXXV, 27, 131. Varro in Gellius, XIV, 7, 7. Cassius Dio, XLIV, 5; XLV, 17; LI, 22. CIL. VI, 877a; 32324, 1718, 32326. Acta Ludorum saecul. Sever., I, 5. Coin of Augustus: Cohen,[2] 122.
Jordan, I, 2, 253. Huelsen, *Röm. Mitt.* 1902, 39–41. Lanciani, *R. and E.,* 263–267; *storia d. scavi* III, 221. Platner, 229f., 238–241.

(P. 30.) SECRETARIUM SENATUS.

CIL. VI, 1718 (=Dessau 5522).
Jordan, I, 2, 257; Lanciani, *Memorie dei Lincei,* XI (1883), 14–21. De Rossi, *Bull. comun.* 1889, 363. Huelsen, *Röm. Mitt.* 1893, 279. Platner, 239.

(P. 32.) BASILICA AEMILIA.

Cicero, *ad Att.* IV, 16, 14. Varro, *L. L.*, VI, 4. Plin., *n.h.* XXXV, 13; XXXVI, 102. Statius, *silv.* I, 1, 22. Tacitus, *hist.* III, 72. Plutarch, *Caes.* 29. Appian, *bell. civ.* II, 26. Cassius Dio, XLIX, 42; LIV, 24. Notitia, reg. IV. Polemius Silvius, 545. CIL, XV, 7189. Coin of Lepidus: Cohen-Babelon, Aemilia n. 25.

Jordan, I, 2, 392. Huelsen, *Röm. Mitt.* 1902, 41–57; 1905, 53–62. Lanciani, *R. and E.*, 237f.; *storia d. scavi* II, 9, 191–193. Platner, 194–199. Toebelmann-Fiechter, *Gebälke*, 27–34.

(P. 34.) SACELLUM (VENERIS) CLOACINAE.

Plautus, *Curculio* IV, 1, 10. Livius, III, 48, 5. Plinius, *n.h.* XV, 119. Coins: Cohen-Babelon, Mussidia n. 6, 7.

Jordan, I, 2, 398. Huelsen, *Röm. Mitt.* 1902, 45; 1905, 62f. Dressel, *Wiener Studien*, 1902, 418f. Platner, 198f.

(P. 34.) PUTEAL LIBONIS (SCRIBONIANUM).

Cicero, *pro Sestio* 18. Horat., *sat.* II, 6, 35; *epist.* I, 19, 8. Ovid, *remed.*, 561. Porphyrio, *ad Horat. epist.* I, 19, 8. Schol. Pers. 4, 49. Festus, 333. Coins: Cohen-Babelon, Aemilia n. 11, Scribonia n. 8, 9.

Benndorf-Schoene, *Lateran* n. 440, p. 307. Jordan, I, 2, 210, 403. Platner, 268. Van Deman, *Am. Jour. Archaeol.*, 1913, 27.

(P. 34.) PORTICUS IULIA.

Schol. Pers., IV, 49.

Van Deman, *American Journal of Archaeology*, 1913, 14–28.

(P. 34.) IANUS.

Livius, I, 49. Ovid, *fast.* I, 257. Cassius Dio, LXXIII, 1. Servius, *ad Aen.* VII, 607. Procop., *de bello Goth.* I, 25. Coins: Cohen, Neron, 153, 161, 178, 183.

Jordan, I, 2, 344–350. Lanciani, *R. and E.*, 254. Platner, 190f. Burchett, *Janus in Roman life and cult* (Menasha, Wis., 1918). H. W. Wright, *American Journal of Archaeology*, 1925, 79–81.

(P. 35.) EQUUS CONSTANTINI.

CIL. VI, 1141 (=Dessau 698). Notita, reg. VIII.

Jordan, I, 2, 189. Lanciani, *R. and E.*, 260. Platner, 262.

(P. 35.) EQUUS DOMITIANI.

Statius, *silv.* I, 1, 21ff.

Jordan, I, 2, 187f. Gatti, *bull. comun.* 1904, 75–82; 174–178. Huelsen, *Röm. Mitt.* 1905, 71–73. Platner, 261f.

SOURCES AND RECENT LITERATURE

(P. 35.) THE CUNICULI.

Huelsen, *Röm. Mitt.* 1902, 57; 1905, 65–67. Platner, 266. Frank, 77.

(P. 35.) FORNIX FABIANUS.

Cicero, *pro Plancio* 17; *in Verrem act.* I, 7, 19; *de oratore* II, 267 with the scholia, p. 133, 393, 399, Orelli. Seneca, *dial.* II, 1, 3. Schol. Pers 4, 49. Histor. August, *vita Salonini* 1. CIL. VI, 1303, 1304 (= Dessau 43).

Jordan, I, 2, 209. Lanciani, *Not. degli scavi* 1882, 222–226; *storia d. scavi* II, 196; *R. and E.* 217f. Huelsen, *Röm. Mitt.*, 1902, 94. Piganiol, *Mélanges de l'Ecole française*, 1908, 89–95. Platner, 319. Van Deman, *Journal of Roman Studies*, 1922, 26f. Clay, *Memoirs of the American Academy*.

(P. 36.) TEMPLUM ANTONINI ET FAUSTINAE.

Histor. August., *vita Pii* 6, 13; *Caracallae* 4; *Salonin.* 1. Notitia, reg. IV. CIL. VI, 1005 (= Dessau 384), 2001. Coin: Cohen, Faustine, 191–194.

Jordan-Huelsen, I, 3, 8. Lanciani, *R. and E.*, 218; *stor. d. scavi* II, 193–195. Platner, 186f. Huelsen, *Chiese di Roma*, p. 288, n. 19. A. Bartoli, *Mon. Ant.* XXIII (1916).

(P. 36.) REGIA.

Ovid, *Trist.* III, 1, 28. Festus, 278, 279. Appian, *bell. civ.* II, 148. Plinius, *epist.* IV, 11. Obsequens 19. FUR. fr. 21. Cassius Dio, fr. 6, 2; XLVIII, 42; LIV, 27. Servius, *ad Aen.* VIII, 363. Solinus, I, 21.

Jordan, I, 2, 302–303; 423–428. Huelsen, *Jahrbuch des Inst.* 1889, 228–253. *CIL.* I², p. 5ff.; *Röm. Mitt.* 1902, 62–66; 1905, 77–80. Lanciani, *R. and E.*, 221–223; *storia d. scavi* II, 197–200. Platner, 210–214. Frank, 4f., 81–85. Toebelmann-Fiechter, *Gebälke*, 1–12.

(P. 37.) TEMPLUM CASTORIS (CASTORUM).

Cicero, *pro Scauro*, 46, and Asconius, ad. l. c., *in Verr.* I, 154. Livius, II, 42. Ovid, *fast.* I, 706. Dionys., VI, 13. Sueton., *Tiber.* 20; *Cal.* 22. Plutarch, *Cato minor*, 27, 28. Cassius Dio, LV, 27; LIX, 23; LX, 6. FUR. fr. 20. Chronogr. a. 354, p. 146, Momms., Notit., reg. VIII.

Jordan, I, 2, 369–376. Lanciani, *R. and E.*, 271–274. Richter, *Jahrbuch des Instituts* 1898, 87–119. Platner, 180f. Huelsen, *Röm. Mitt.* 1902, 66f.; 1905, 80. Van Deman, *American Journal of Archaeology*, 1912, 244. Frank, 78. Toebelmann-Fiechter, *Gebälke*, 51. Frank, *Memoirs of the American Academy in Rome*, V (1925).

(P. 38). LACUS IUTURNAE.

Ovid, *fast.* I, 706. Dionysius, VI, 13. Coin: Cohen-Babelon, Postumia n. 5, 6.

Jordan, I, 2, 371. Lanciani, *storia d. scavi* II, 202. Boni, *Not. d. scavi* 1901, 41–144. Huelsen, *Röm. Mitt.* 1902, 67–73; 1905 81f. Platner, 214–219. Frank, 76.

(P. 39.) Aedicula Minervae.

Martial, IV, 53, 1, 2. Chronogr. a. 354, p. 146, Momms. Curios. reg. VIII (Notit. om.). Diplomata honestae missionis, n. XXIIff. (from Domitian to Diocletian).

Mommsen, *CIL.* IIIS. p. 2035. Huelsen, I, 3, 84.

(P. 40.) Bibliotheca Templi Divi Augusti.

Plinius, *n.h.,* XXXIV, 43. Sueton., *Tiber.,* 74. Martial, XII, 3, 7.

Huelsen, *Topogr.* I, 3, 82; *Forum,* 172f. Platner, 162f. Delbrueck, *Jahrbuch des Instituts* 1921, 8–31.

(P. 40.) S. Maria Antiqua.

Huelsen, *Röm. Mitt.* 1902, 83–88; 1905, 84–91. Rushforth, *Papers of the British School at Rome,* I (1902), p. 1–123. De Grueneisen, *Sainte Marie Antique* (Rome, 1911). Marucchi, *Églises et basiliques de Rome,* 247. Wilpert, *Mosaiken und Malereien* I, II, *passim.* Huelsen, *Chiese di Roma,* p. 309, n. 8.

(P. 43.) Templum Divi Augusti.

Sueton., *Tiber,* 47; *Caligula* 21, 22; *Galba* 1. Acta Arvalium A. D. 39ff. (Henzen, p. 55). Plinius, *n.h.* XII, 94; *XXXV,* 131. Tacitus, *ann.* VI, 45. Cassius Dio, LVI, 46; LVII, 10; LIX, 7. Coins of Caligula: Cohen, n. 9–11; of Antoninus Pius, Cohen, n. 1–12; 618; 797–810. CIL. VI, 4222 (=Orelli 2446), 8704.

Lanciani, *R. and E.,* 122–125. Huelsen, *Röm. Mitt.* 1902, 74–82; 1905, 82f.; *Topogr.* I, 3, 80f. Platner, 161f. Delbrueck, *Jahrbuch des Instituts,* 1921, 8–31.

(P. 43.) Horrea Agrippiana.

Notit. reg. VIII. CIL. VI, 9972 (=Dessau 7971), 10026; XIV, 3958 (=Dessau 7572). Inscription Bull. comun. 1914, p. 29. FUR. fr. 37 + 86. Jordan, I, 2, 472. Huelsen, *Röm. Mitt.* 1905, 84. Schneider-Graziosi, *Bull. comun.,* 1911, 158–172; 1914, 25–33.

(P. 44.) Aedes Vestae.

Varro, ap. Gellium XIV, 7, 7. Livius, epit. 19. Horatius, *sat.* I, 9, 8. Dionys., II, 66. Ovid, *fast.* VI, 265; 437–454; *trist.* III, 1, 27. Tacitus, *ann.* XV, 41. Plinius *n.h.* VII, 141. Plutarch, *Numa* 11; *Herodian,* I, 14, 4. Cassius Dio, LXXII, 24. Orosius, IV, 19. Notitia, reg. VIII. For the coins see: Dressel, *Zeitschrift für Numismatik,* 1899, 20–31.

Jordan, I, 2, 293; 421–431; *Tempel der Vesta* (1886). Auer, *Denkschriften der*

Wiener Akademie, 1888, 209–228. Lanciani, *R. and E.,* 225–228; *stor. d. scavi* II, 203. Boni, *Not. d. scavi,* 1900, 159–191. Altmann, *Italische Rundbauten,* 14, 51. Platner, 200–204.

(P. 46.) ATRIUM VESTAE.

Ovid, *fast.* VI, 263. Festus, 333. Gellius, I, 12, 9. Plinius, *ep.* VII, 19. Servius, *ad Aen.* VII, 153. Prudentius *peristeph.* II, 528. CIL. VI, 32409–32428 (= Dessau 4924–4938).

Jordan, I, 2, 299, 427; *Tempel der Vesta* (1886), 25–40. Lanciani, *R. and E.,* 228–254; *storia d. scavi* II, 203. Auer, *Denkschriften der Wiener Akademie,* 1888, II, 206–228. Van Deman, *American Journal of Archaeology,* 1904, 324; *The Atrium Vestae* (Washington, 1909). Huelsen, *Röm. Mitt.,* 1902, 90–92; 1905, 94. Platner, 204–210.

(P. 48.) TEMPLUM DIVI ROMULI.

CIL. VI, 1147. Coins: Cohen VII, p. 182, n. 6–12.

Lanciani, *R. and E.,* 211–213; *storia d. scavi* II, 59; III, 222. Huelsen, I, 3, 10. Platner, 337f. Biasiotti and Whitehead, *Rendiconti dell' Accad. Pontificia III* (1924–25), 83–122.

(P. 48.) BIBLIOTHECA TEMPLI PACIS.

Gellius, V, 21, 9; XVI, 8, 2.

Lanciani, *bull. comun,* 1882, 22–54; *R. and E.,* 213–217. Huelsen, I, 3, 4–6. Biasiotti and Whitehead, *Rendiconti dell' Accad. Pontificia* III (1924–25), p. 83–122.

(P. 49.) BASILICA CONSTANTINI.

Notitia reg. IV et app. Aurel. Victor, *Caes.,* 40. Chronogr. a. 354, p. 146, Mommsen. Polemius Silvius, 545.

Lanciani, *R. and E.,* 203–208. Huelsen I, 3, 11–14. Platner, 335f.

(P. 51.) HORREA PIPERATARIA.

Cassius Dio, LXXII, 24. Chronogr. a. 354, p. 146, Momms.

Lanciani, *bull. comun.,* 1900, 8–13. Huelsen I, 3, 7. Platner, 312.

(P. 51.) TEMPLUM VENERIS ET ROMAE.

Cassius Dio, LXIX, 4; LXXI, 31. Hist. Aug., *vita Hadrian,* 19. Athenaeus VIII, 63, p. 361. Aur. Victor, *Caes,* 40. Notit., reg. IV. Chronogr. a. 354, p. 146, Momms. Ammianus Marcellin., XVI, 10, 14. Servius, *in Aen.* II, 227. Prudentius, *contra Symmach.,* I, 214. Coins: Cohen, Antonin, 698–703; 1074–1076. Relief: Matz-Duhn, 3519; Benndorf-Schoene, *Lateran,* 20. Petersen, *Röm. Mitt.,* 1895, 248.

Lanciani, *R. and E.;* 196–200, *storia d. scavi* 220–222. Huelsen, I, 3, 17–20. Platner, 326.

(P. 52.) COLOSSUS NERONIS.

Sueton., *Nero,* 31; *Vespasian,* 18. Plinius, *n.h.* XXXIV, 45. Martial, *de spect.* 2, *epigr.* I, 70, 6. Cassius Dio, LXVI, 15, 1; LXXII, 22, 3. Histor. August., *vita Hadriani,* 19; *Commodi* 17. Herodian I, 15, 9. Notitia, reg. IV. Hieronym. ad. a. Abr. 2090 (2091). Hemerol. Filocal. ad VIII id. Iun. CIL. VIII, 212, 82 (=Buecheler *Anth.* L. 1552). Beda Venerabilis, *collect.* 1, III (Migne, PL. XCIV, 543).

Huelsen, I, 3, 320f. *Bull. comun.* 1926. Fr. Marx, *Wiener Studien,* XX, 177. Platner, 335.

(P. 52.) ARCUS TITI.

CIL. VI, 945 (=Dessau, 265).

Lanciani, *R. and E.,* 201–203. Huelsen, I, 3, 15, 16. Curtis, *Suppl. Papers of the American School at Rome* II, 47. Platner, 319–322. Frothingham, *American Journal of Archaeology,* XVIII (1914), 479–483.

(P. 59.) FICUS RUMINALIS.

Varro, *L. L.,* V, 54. Livius, I, 4, 5; X, 23, 12. Ovid, *fast.* II, 412. Festus, 270, 271. Plutarch, *Romul.,* 4. Plinius, *n.h.* XV, 77. Servius, *ad Aen.* VIII, 90.

Huelsen, I, 3, 38. Platner, 129f.

(P. 59.) LUPERCAL.

Cicero, *ad fam.* VII, 26. Livius, I, 5, 1. Vergil, *Aen.* VIII, 343. Monum. Ancyr., IV, 2. CIL. VI, 912b, 31200. Ovid, *fast.* V, 375ff. Dionys., I, 32, 3; 79, 8. Velleius, I, 15. Servius, *ad Aen.* VIII, 90, 343. Notitia, reg. X. Clemes Alexandr., *strom.,* I, 21, p. 139, Sylburg.

Huelsen, I, 3, 37. Platner, 92, 130. A. M. Franklin, *The Lupercalia* (New York, 1921).

(P. 59.) CASA ROMULI (TUGURIUM FAUSTULI).

Argei *ap Varron., L. L.,* V, 54. Dionys. I, 79, 11. Plutarch, *Romul.,* 20. Cassius Dio XLVIII, 43; LIV, 29. Solin. I, 18. Notitia, reg. X. Hieronymus, *praef. in libros Didymi de spiritu sancto* (22, 105 ed. Vallarsi).

Huelsen, I, 3, 39. Platner, 130.

(P. 60.) ROMA QUADRATA.

Ennius, ap. Festum, 254. Varro, ap. Solin. I, 17. Plutarch, *Romul.,* 9. Dionys., I, 88; II, 65. Appian, frg. 7, 4.

Huelsen, I, 3, 35f. Platner, *American Journal of Philology,* 1901, 420f. Carter, *American Journal of Archaeology,* 1908, 172–183. Täubler, *Röm. Mitt.,* 1926, 212–226.

SOURCES AND RECENT LITERATURE

(P. 60.) PORTA ROMANA (ROMANULA).

Varro *L. L.,* V, 164; VI, 24. Festus, 262.
Jordan, I, 1, 176. Platner, 38, 134; *Classical Philology,* 1917, 196.

(P. 60.) PORTA MUGONIA (VETUS PALATII).

Varro, *L. L.,* V, 164. Livius I, 12, 3, 9. Dionys. II, 50. Paulus ex Festo, 144. Nonius, 531. Solin., I, 24.
Jordan, I, 1, 174. Platner, 37.

(P. 60.) PRIMITIVE FORTIFICATIONS OF THE HILL.

Jordan, I, 1, 172f. Huelsen, I, 3, 37. Richter, *Annali dell'Instituto,* 1884, 189–204. Lanciani, *R. and E.,* 59, 128. Platner, 131f. Frank, 91f.

(P. 60.) SCALAE CACI.

Diodor., IV, 21, 2. Plutarch, *Romul.,* 20. Solin., I, 17.
Jordan, I, 2, 482. Huelsen, I, 3, 39f. Platner, 133f. Frank, 98f.

(P. 60.) REMAINS BETWEEN THE SCALAE CACI AND THE DOMUS LIVIAE.

Lanciani, *R. and E.,* 128–132. Huelsen, I, 3, 42. Vaglieri, *Notizie d. scavi,* 1907, 185–205, 264–282, 444–460, 529–542. Pinza, *Annali della Società degli Ingegneri ed Architetti,* 1907. Pigorini, *Rendiconti dei Lincei,* 1907, 669–680; 1908, 201–210; 1909, 249–262. Platner, 132f. Frank, 98f.

(P. 61.) ARA AII LOCUTII.

Cicero, *de divin.* I, 101; II, 69. Varro, ap. Gell. XVI, 17. Livius V, 32, 6; 50, 5; 52, 11. Plutarch, *Camill.* 14, 30; *de fort Romanor.,* 5.
Lanciani, *R. and E.,* 128. Huelsen, I, 3, 46. Platner, 141.

(P. 61.) ARA SEXTI CALVINI.

CIL. I, 623; VI, 110, 30701 (=Dessau, 4015).
Lanciani, *R. and E.,* 128. Huelsen, I, 3, 47. Platner, 141.

(P. 61.) TEMPLUM VICTORIAE.

Livius, X, 33, 9; XXXIX, 9, 6. Dionys., I, 32, 5. CIL. VI, 31059, 31060. Hemerol. Praenestin, *Eph. epigr.,* IX, n. 740, ad kal. Aug.; Hemerol. Antiat., *Not. d. scavi,* 1921, 104 ad kal. Aug.
Lanciani, *R. and E.,* 126f. Huelsen, I, 3, 47f. Platner, 138. Mancini, *Not. d. scavi,* 1921, l. c.

THE FORUM AND THE PALATINE

(P. 61.) Templum Iovis Victoris.

Livius, X, 29, 14; 42, 7. Ioseph., *Ant. iud.* XIX, 4, 3. Ovid, *fast.,* IV, 621. Cassius Dio, XLVII, 40, 2, cf. XLV, 17, 2; LX, 35, 1. Notit., reg. X. Hemerol. Antiat., *Not d. scavi,* 1921, p. 92 ad id. April.

Lanciani, *R. and E.,* 138. Huelsen, I, 3, 50. Platner, 142; *Bull. comun.,* 1917, 84–89. Frank, 92–94.

(P. 61.) Aedes Magnae Matris.

Cicero, *de har. resp.,* 24. Livius, XXIX, 37, 2; XXXVI, 36, 3. Valer. Max., I, 8, 11. Ovid, *fast.,* II, 55; IV, 347. Monum. Ancyr., IV, 8. Iuvenal, IX, 23. Martial, VII, 73. Cassius Dio, XLVIII, 43, 4. Obseq. 39 (99). Histor. Aug., *vita Claudii* 4; *Aurelian.* 1. Auct., *de vir. ill.* 46, 7. Notit. reg. X. Fasti Praen. ad April, 10; Fasti minor. CIL. I^2, p. 251, n. V. Hemerol. Antiat, *Not. d. scavi,* 1921, 91. CIL. VI, 496, 1040, 30967, 32498; XII, 405.

Lanciani, *R. and E.,* 134–138. Huelsen I, 3, 51. Esdaile, *Röm. Mitt.,* 1908, 368–374. Graillot, *Bibl. des Ecoles franç.* CVII, 320–326. Platner, 139. Frank, 96f. Toebelmann-Fiechter, *Gebälke,* 5.

(P. 63.) Domus M. Ciceronis.

Cicero, *de domo* 37, 62, 103, 114, 116; *de harusp. respons.* 6, 8, 15; *in Pison.,* 11; *pro Plancio,* 7; *ad Attic.* II, 24; IV, 1; 2, 5; 3, 2; *ad fam.* V, 6, 2. Velleius, II, 14, 3; 45, 3. Plutarch, Cic. 8, 22, 33. Appian. *bell, civ.* II, 15. Gellius, XII, 2. Cassius Dio, XXXVIII, 17, 6; XXXIX, 11, 1; 20, 3. Ps. Sall. in Cic. 2, 2; Ps. Cicero in Sallust. 5, 14; 7, 20.

Huelsen, I, 3, 58f.

(P. 63.) Domus Liviae.

Inscriptions on lead pipes, CIL. XV, 7264, 7285.

Lanciani *R. and E.,* 149–151. Huelsen, I, 3, 61. Platner, 135–137. The frescoes: *Monumenti dell'Instituto,* XI, tav. 22, 23. Mau, *Geschichte der Wandmalerei,* Tf. 9; cf. Mau, *Annali dell'Instituto,* 1880, 136ff.; *Geschichte der Wandmalerei,* 167–174, 196–205.

(P. 65.) Templum Apollinis.

Monum. Ancyr. IV, 1, 24; 54. Vitruv., III, 3, 4. Propert., II, 23, 29; III, 31; IV, 1, 3; 6, 11, 17, 67. Vergil, *Aen.* VIII, 704. Ovid, *met.* XIII, 715; *fast.* IV, 951. Festus, 258. Velleius, II, 81. Sueton., *Aug.,* 29; *Nero,* 25. Tacit., *hist.* I, 27; III, 65. Iosephus, *bell. iud.* I, 2, 6, 1. Plinius, *n.h.* XXXIV, 14; XXXV, 24, 25, 32, 100; XXXVI, 13; XXXVII, 11. Cassius Dio, XLIX, 15, 5; LIII, 1, 3. Ascon., in Ciceron, *in toga cand.,* p. 90, Or. Servius. *ad Aen.* VIII, 704. Notit., reg. X. Hist. Augusta, *vita Claudi Goth.* 4. Ammian. Marcellin. XXIII, 3, 3; 6, 24. Acta ludorum saecul. Aug. CIL. VI, 32323, 32, 139; Sever. CIL. VI, 32327, 723; Hemerol. Arval. Amiternin. Antiat. ad VII id. Octobr.

Lanciani, *R. and E.*, 141, 145. Huelsen, I, 3, 66, *Geogr. Jahrbuch* XXXIV (Göttingen, 1911) 20; *Dissertat. dell' Accad. Pontificia,* ser. II, tom. XI (1914), 116f. Bartoli, *Nuovo Bullettino di Archeologia cristiana,* 1907, 191f. Pinza, *Bull. comun.,* 1910, 3–41; 1913, 199–224. Platner, 144–147.

(P. 65.) BIBLIOTHECA APOLLINIS.

Ovid, *trist.* III, 1, 63. Horat., *epist.,* I, 3, 17, with the scholia. Sueton., *Aug.* 29. Plinius, *n.h.* VII, 210; XXXIV, 43. Tacitus, *ann.* II, 37, 83. Plinius, *epist.* I, 1, 13. Fronto, *epist.* IV, 5. Galen., *de comp. medic.* I, 1 (XII, 362, ed. Kuehn). Cassius Dio, LIII, 1, 3. Servius, *ad ecl.,* 4, 10. CIL. VI, 5186–5191, 5884.

Huelsen, I, 3, 71. Platner 146.

(P. 66.) AREA PALATINA.

Josephus, *ant. iud.* XIX, 3, 1. Gellius, XX, 1, 1. Notitia, reg. X (Curiosum om.). Huelsen, I, 3, 66. Pinza, *Bull. comun.,* 1910, 3f. Platner, 165.

(P. 66.) TEMPLUM IOVIS STATORIS.

Cicero, *in Catilin.,* I, 11, 33; II, 12. Ps.-Cireco, *antequam iret in exilium,* 24. Ovid, *fast.* VI, 793; *trist.* III, 1, 31. Livius, I, 12, 6; 41, 4; X, 36, 11; 37, 15; XXXVII, 37, 7. Dionys., II, 50. Plinius, *n.h.* XXXIV, 29. Appian, *bell. civ.,* II, 11. Plutarch, *Cicero,* 16. Memerol. Antiat. *Not. d. scavi,* 1921, p. 111, Sept. 5. The relief of the Haterii tomb: *Monumenti dell'Instituto.* V, tav. 7.

Lanciani, *R. and E.,* 200f. Huelsen, I, 3, 20–23. Platner, 313; *Bul. comun.,* 1917, 79–84.

(P. 67.) DOMUS TIBERIANA.

Tacitus, *hist.* I, 27; II, 85. Sueton., *Otho,* 6. Gellius, XIII, 19, 1. Plutarch, *Galba,* 24. Hist. Aug., *vita Antonin. Pii* 10; *Marci* 6; *Veri* 2, 6; *Probi,* 2. Notit., reg. X. CIL. VI, 8653–8655.

Lanciani, *R. and E.,* 151–157. Huelsen, *Röm. Mitt.,* 1895, 296f; *Topogr.* I, 3, 76. Platner, 147, 148, 159–161.

(P. 68.) DOMUS AUGUSTIANA.

Monum. Ancyran. VI, 13, 24. Ovid, *trist.* III, 1, 27. Sueton., *Aug.* 57, 72, 73. Tacitus, *histor.,* III, 68. Cassius Dio, LIII, 16, 4; LIV, 27, 3; LV, 12, 4. Notit., reg. X. Hemerol. Praenestin. ad idus Ianuar. and IV. kal. Mai. CIL. VI, 2271, 8640–8646, 8649–8651; CIL. XV, 1860, 7246.

Lanciani, *R. and E.*, 139–145. Huelsen I, 3, 65, 74f. Pinza, *bull. comun.,* 1910, 30f. Boni, *Journal of Roman Studies,* 1913, 246f.

(P. 72.) THE SO-CALLED PAEDAGOGIUM.

Inscriptions in Garrucci, *Graffiti de Pompéi* (Paris, 1856) pl. XII, XXV, XXX, XXXI. Correra, *Bull. comun.*, 1893, 249; 1894, 92.

Huelsen I, 3, 92; *Mélanges Boissier,* 1903, 301–306; *Papers of the British School at Rome,* VIII, 91–103.

(P. 74.) HIPPODROMUS PALATII.

Acta S. Sebastiani (AA. SS. Jan. 20, vol. I, p. 278, 642).

Barnabei, Cozza and Gatti, *Monumenti dei Lincei* V, (1895), 16–83. Marx, *Jahrbuch des Instituts,* 1895, 129–143. Huelsen, *Röm. Mitt.*, 1895, 276–283; *Top.* I, 3, 94, 97. Lanciani, *R. and E.*, 174–180. Haugwitz, *Palatin,* 80f. and Fig. 10. Platner, 154–157.

(P. 75.) REMAINS BETWEEN THE HIPPODROMUS AND S. BONAVENTURA.

Deglane, *Mélanges de l'École franç.*, 1888, 199–205. Huelsen I, 3, 97.

(P. 75.) SEPTIZONIUM SEVERI.

CIL. VI, 1032, 31229. Hist. Aug., *vita Severi,* 24. FUR. fr. 38. Notit., reg. X. Chronogr., a. 354, p. 147, Mommsen. Ammian. Marcellin., XV, 7, 3.

Huelsen, *das Septizonium des Severus* (Berlin, 1886); *Topogr.* I, 3, 100; *Zeitschrift für Geschichte der Architektur,* 1911, 1–24. Lanciani, *R. and E.*, 183f.; *Storia d. scavi* II, 51–54; IV, 137–139. Bartoli, *Bolletino d'Arte,* 1909, 253–269. Platner, 157f. Dombart, *Das palatinische Septizonium,* München, 1922. Archäol. Anzeiger, 1923–24, 41.

INDEX

INDEX

INDEX

Note: The long axis of the Forum runs about from N. W. to S. E., but for the sake of simplicity in the text the northeast side (with the Basilica Aemilia) is referred to as the north side, and the southwest side (with the Basilica Julia), as the south side. Similarly, the four corners of the Palatine correspond approximately to the four cardinal points of the compass: the east corner lies opposite the Colosseum, the north corner toward the Forum, the west corner toward the Tiber and the south corner opposite the Aventine.

The Necropolis at the Velia

Excavations near the Arch of Severus
(Tomb of Romulus)

Phot. Anderson

Tullianum — Present Condition

Phot. Anderson

The Forum Seen from the East

Phot. Anderson

The Forum Seen from the West

Façade of the Basilica Julia towards the Forum

Phot. Anderson

Temples of Saturn and Vespasian

Phot. Alinari

PORTICUS DEORUM CONSENTIUM

Temple of Vespasian — Reconstructed

Phot. Alinari

Cornice of the Temple of Concord

Phot. Alinari

Cornice of the Temple of Vespasian

Phot. Vasari

Arch of Septimius Severus

Phot. Vasari

The Column of Phocas

Phot. Anderson

Façade of the Curia (S. Adriano)

Phot. Anderson

TEMPLUM ANTONINI ET FAUSTINÆ

Phot. Anderson

Remains of the Regia

Phot. Anderson

Remains of the Temple of Castor

Phot. Anderson

LACUS IUTURNAE

Phot. Anderson

BIBLIOTHECA TEMPLI DIVI AUGUSTI
(S. Maria Antiqua)

Phot. Anderson

Fresco from S. Maria Antiqua

Phot. Anderson

Fresco from S. Maria Antiqua

Phot. Anderson

TEMPLUM DIVI AUGUSTI

Phot. Anderson

AEDICULA VESTAE

Phot. Anderson

ATRIUM VESTAE

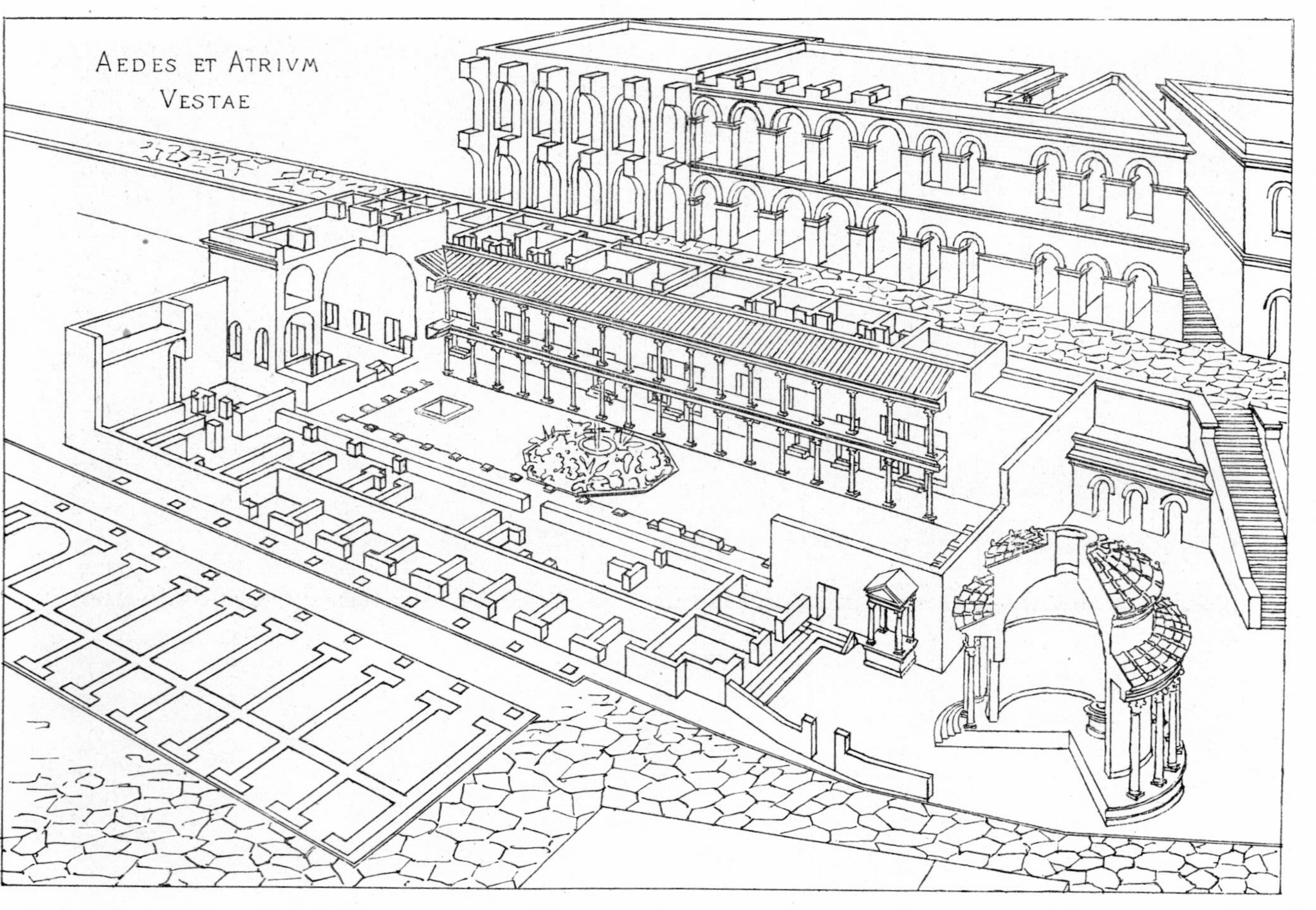

The Temple of Vesta and the House of the Vestals — Reconstructed

Phot. Anderson

TEMPLUM DIVI ROMULI

Phot. Vasari

Remains of the Basilica of Constantine

The Temple of Romulus and the Basilica of Constantine about 1550

Phot. Anderson

TEMPLUM VENERIS ET ROMAE

Phot. Vasari

Arch of Titus

The Forum in the XVIIIth Century

The Forum in the Year 1824

The Forum in the Year 1860

The Forum in the Year 1881

The Forum in the Year 1898

Phot. Anderson

The Hut of Romulus

Temple of Jupiter Victor

DOI

Phot. Anderson

TEMPLUM MAGNAE MATRIS

Phot. Anderson

Cryptoporticus in the Palace of Tiberius

AREA PALATINA

Phot. Anderson

North Corner of the Palatine

Phot. Alinari

Stuccoes in the Cryptoporticus

Phot. Vasari

Remains of the Palace of the Flavians

Phot. Vasari

So-called Basilica in the Palace of the Flavians

Phot. Alinari

Fountain in the Triclinium

Phot. Alinari

Arched Passage in the Palace of Severus

Stairway to the Upper Story of the Palace of Severus

Phot. Alinari

The Palace of Severus as Seen from the Aventine

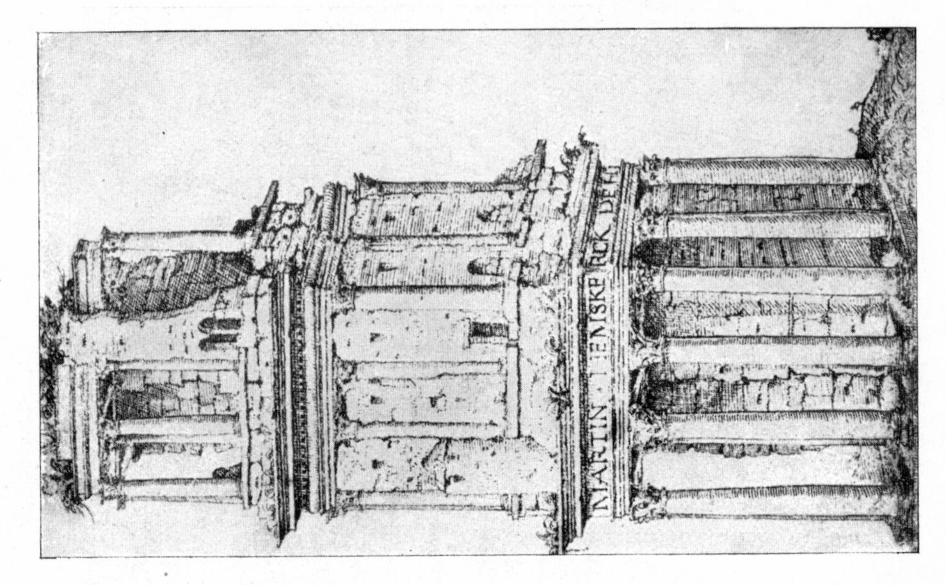

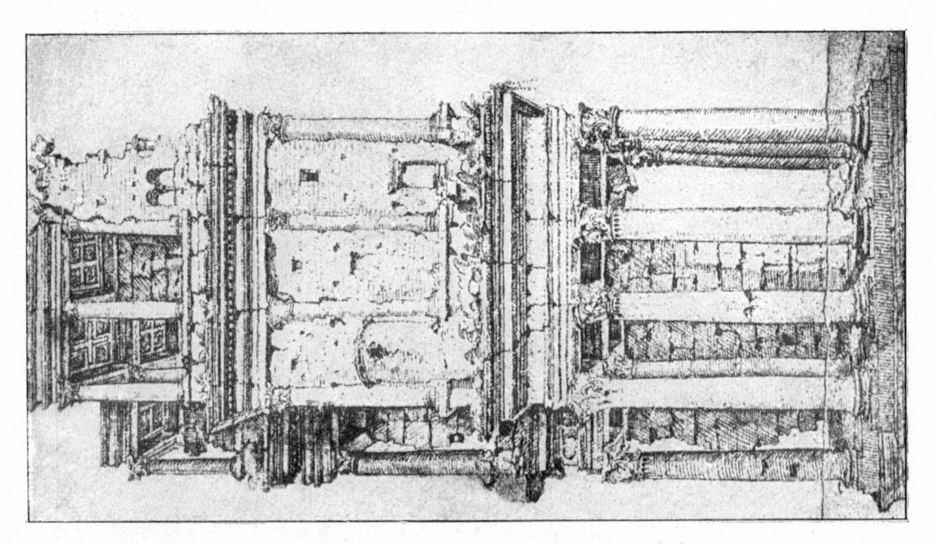

Remains of the Septizonium in the First Half of the XVIth Century

The Farnese Gardens in the XVIIIth Century

Entrance to the Farnese Gardens about 1880